INITIATION SCIENCE

and the Development of the Human Mind

INITIATION SCIENCE

and the Development of the Human Mind

Eight lectures and a report on a visit to Britain
given in Dornach, London and Stuttgart between 27 July and 16 September 1923

TRANSLATED BY ANNA MEUSS

INTRODUCTION BY ANNA MEUSS

RUDOLF STEINER

RUDOLF STEINER PRESS

CW 228

The publishers gratefully acknowledge the generous funding of this publication by the estate of Dr Eva Frommer MD (1927–2004) and the Anthroposophical Society in Great Britain

Rudolf Steiner Press
Hillside House, The Square
Forest Row, RH18 5ES

www.rudolfsteinerpress.com

Published by Rudolf Steiner Press 2016

Originally published in German under the title *Initiationswissenschaft und Sternenerkenntnis. Der Mensch in Vergangenheit, Gegenwart und Zukunft vom Gesichtspunkt der Bewußtseinsentwickelung* (volume 228 in the *Rudolf Steiner Gesamtausgabe* or Collected Works) by Rudolf Steiner Verlag, Dornach. Based on shorthand notes that were not reviewed or revised by the speaker. This authorized translation is based on latest available (third) edition (2002), edited by Hella Wiesberger and Michaelis Messmer

Sketches within the text based on Rudolf Steiner's blackboard drawings by Assya Turgenev

Published by permission of the Rudolf Steiner Nachlassverwaltung, Dornach

© Rudolf Steiner Nachlassverwaltung, Dornach, Rudolf Steiner Verlag 2002

This translation © Rudolf Steiner Press 2016

A catalogue record for this book is available from the British Library

ISBN 978 1 85584 531 2

Cover by Mary Giddens
Typeset by DP Photosetting, Neath, West Glamorgan
Printed and bound by Gutenberg Press Ltd., Malta

CONTENTS

LECTURE 2

DORNACH, 28 JULY 1923

From Newton's day onwards, the spiritual way of looking at the heavenly bodies has been lost. Mathematical and physical concepts have since been extended to the whole of the heavens. Einstein's theory of relativity destroys these popular concepts. In anthroposophy, a moral world order takes the place of physical concepts. Example: spirits that have withdrawn into the interior of the moon have brought about the spinal column in man and animal. Ancient oriental wisdom—now in decline—survives outwardly in a soulful view of the universe. Ramanathan's criticism of European understanding of the New Testament. Europeans need to read the Gospels without bias to find a spiritual Christ. Over the last three or four centuries a tendency to be vague has clouded all concepts. Ultimately this is also the cause of the social chaos.

pages 16–30

LECTURE 3

DORNACH, 29 JULY 1923

Man and animal and the waking, sleeping and dreaming levels of conscious awareness. Differences in the way man and animal relate to the inner and outside world. Natural science reckons according to weight, measure and number, and does not know what to do with sensory perceptions. Sensory perceptions (sound, colour, heat, cold) are free from weight, measure and number, and have the opposite of gravity. Human beings come to understand spiritual entities by being aware of this urge to expand. In the waking state, human beings see only the outer aspect of the natural worlds; in sleep they are with the spiritual element inherent in those worlds. In sleep human beings live with the concepts of earthly truth. Sentience of beauty and the dream. Preconditions for seeing the chaos. Beauty arises when chaos changes into cosmos, which is the case with anything artistic. The idea of goodness (the good) in connection with the difference between inner world and outside world and the waking state. Theory of relativity and reality. Materialistic science repudiates anything to do with art. Icons, images of the Madonna and the weightlessness of colour (reference to his own paintings on programmes). Warnings about issues in the Anthroposophical Society.

pages 31–49

Part Two
MAN AS THE IMAGE OF COSMIC SPIRITS AND THEIR ACTIVITIES

LECTURE 4
LONDON, 2 SEPTEMBER 1923

The things that happen to man in sleep are more important than anything that happens during waking hours. If people did not sleep they would not be in a position to do things deliberately. The influence of higher hierarchies in man during waking hours and sleep. The outer form of the human being reflects the activities of all the hierarchies within him. Lower spirituality takes effect through the mineral, vegetable and animal worlds on earth; the influences of higher spirituality on man come through the world of stars. The moon—externally—reflecting physical and spiritual impulses coming from the universe. Inside the moon live the former teachers of original wisdom on earth. They continue to be active in the physical powers of procreation for man and animal. Saturn is the cosmic I of the planetary system, preserving cosmic memory and mediating human karma. The other planets and their activities are between the moon, which mediates physical heredity, and Saturn, which mediates karma. Connections between Mars and Venus enter into human organs of speech and song on earth. From the time when Gnostic wisdom on earth was lost, the Mystery on Golgotha gives us the power to gain awareness of what is happening in the worlds of the stars. Human beings must learn to see themselves again as an image of spirits and spiritual activities on earth.

pages 53–66

Part Three
REPORT ON MY VISIT TO ENGLAND [AND WALES] AND THE WORK DONE THERE

REPORT ON MY VISIT TO ENGLAND [AND WALES] AND THE WORK DONE THERE
DORNACH, 9 SEPTEMBER 1923

The atmosphere at Ilkley. Need for spiritual impulses to come into our present civilization. Signs engraved in stones by Druid priests. Waldorf School education considered against the historical evolution of education. Review of eurythmy performances and contributions made by teachers from Stuttgart Waldorf School.

Penmaenmawr. Position of the town and traces of past Druid ministry. Ritual sites. Druid circles. Wales as preserver of spiritual life. Miss McMillan and her teaching establishment. Presenting medicines at the lectures given for 40 physicians in London. Final eurythmy performance at Royal Academy of Art. Reference to the spread of a general state of sleep in our culture.

Part Four

THE DRUID PRIEST'S SUN INITIATION AND HIS
PERCEPTION OF THE MOON SPIRITS

LECTURE 5
DORNACH, 10 SEPTEMBER 1923

Sun spirits, previously connected with evolution on earth, now live outside the earth. An unconscious memory remained for mankind of the teachers of original wisdom who today live inside the moon. These memories come up in different developmental periods of a sun-type and a moon-type civilization. The Druid priests investigated the secrets of the universe in their cromlechs. On their own, sun powers make cells proliferate; configuration and variety depend on moon powers working together with the sun powers. Elemental spirits sought to grow into giants—those from the root sphere into frost giants, enormously enlarged elements from leaf growth into gales with fog, and giant growth from the flower sphere into devastating fires. Meteorological events were perceived to be powers that lived in the natural worlds and had grown to giant size. The Druid priests' knowledge influenced social and religious life. Observing the plants, the giants and the nature spirits the priests gained insights which enabled them to produce medicines. This civilization existed in parts of northern and central Europe. The written word did not yet exist. It was Woden—with impulses coming from Mercury—who brought runes and thus the first intellectualistic impact. The legend of Baldur shows intellectualism to be the state of mind which reckons with death but knows no remedy for death. Following the Mystery on Golgotha, the fear of death connected with this can be healed in mind and spirit with the figure of the Christ which[*] is able to rise from death.

---

[*] The text definitely says 'which' and not 'who', thus referring to 'figure'. A thinking point.

Part Five
THE PAST, PRESENT AND FUTURE DEVELOPMENT OF THE HUMAN MIND

LECTURE 6
STUTTGART, 14 SEPTEMBER 1923

Human sentience of historical evolution calls for inclusion not only of the present but also of the time that has gone before. Occidental philosophies put more emphasis on time, oriental philosophies on space. The evolution of the mind is the most important factor in human evolution. Forming of ideas, feeling and will intent and the experience of their essential nature when waking, dreaming and sleeping. Human thinking changed from the fifteenth century onwards and has reached its high point today. Human beings lose themselves in present-day scientific thinking. Things that are true on earth cannot be considered analogous and applied to the cosmos, just as truth of the heavenly spheres must not be applied to earth. The Druid priests perceived the cosmic influences and arranged social and economic tasks to be in accord with these. The ground plan for the stone circles near Penmaenmawr is like that of the First Goetheanum. The Druid priests knew how the cosmos influenced plant and animal. They controlled elemental spirits and utilized this knowledge to produce medicines. Jacob Boehme's and Swedenborg's ways of thinking were genuine memories of earlier lives on earth.

pages 105–120

LECTURE 7
STUTTGART, 15 SEPTEMBER 1923

The three stages of evolution for the human mind. Our present three states of conscious awareness in waking, dreaming and sleeping have taken the place of a conscious awareness of images—not ideas—in earlier times. Observation using only the senses started when human beings felt that they had been cast out from the spiritual world (the Fall). Mysteries shone out to people, offering comfort. The priest of the mysteries and the insights he gained from waking dreams, sleep as the cup of oblivion and from embracing the earth (in sleep). The earth's forces of attraction are counteracted by moon forces (negative gravity). A priest in the mysteries was able to raise his spirit to the starry heavens. He taught the influence of the starry environment on human beings on earth (astrological initiation). The priests in the mysteries thus guided humanity back to the spirit in nature. As the spirituality experienced in the old states of mind deteriorated, the impulse of freedom came through the Mystery on Golgotha. Somnambulism is an atavistic effect of moon powers. The works of Jacob Boehme contain atavistic sun effects (the revelation of inner secrets of nature). More profound influences than those of sun and moon come from the planets, from Saturn as cosmic and historic memory. The powers of Saturn that have come alive in Swedenborg.

LECTURE 8
STUTTGART, 16 SEPTEMBER 1923

A sensory perception (or thought process) needs two to four days to be impressed in ether body and physical body so that it may be a memory. Physical body and ether body belong wholly to the cosmos. The significance of three days needed for initiation in earlier times. Dream events as protest against natural laws. Staudenmaier's experiments in spiritualism. Moral world order in opposition to natural science. Human experiences are imprinted in a moral world order after about three days. Evolution of conscious awareness as consequence of the Mystery on Golgotha. From the fifteenth century onwards, the moral world order ranks as 'belief' for the modern mind (reference to Fischer's logarithm anecdote). Nervousness reflecting a future change in the human organization. Future states of mind are dull dream sleep, waking state, hyper-awareness. Present-day scientific logic and its illusions contrasted with the truth of life. Humanity will need a new spirituality so that they do not fall into decadence where the future states of mind are concerned. About the discussion on the next day. The whole *anthropos* as the human being in past, present and future.

INTRODUCTION

The year 1923 proved to be a hard one for Rudolf Steiner. It began with the fire which destroyed the First Goetheanum on New Year's Eve and New Year's Day. Rudolf Steiner made great efforts to sound a positive note in the face of this and also in response to the growing opposition to and enmity against anthroposophy. He travelled extensively, mostly between Dornach and anthroposophical centres in Germany, and did a lot of work for the Waldorf School movement, the priests, the furthering of the arts, especially eurythmy, and the establishment of new branches of the Anthroposophical Society.

Looking at July 1923, we find that on the first day of that month Rudolf Steiner attended a meeting of the School Society to discuss the founding of a school in Basel, and at 5 p.m. a eurythmy performance. At 8 p.m. he gave a lecture for members (in CW 225). The next day he made the pastel sketch *Man in the Spirit* and then went to Stuttgart. There he visited the Waldorf School in the morning. In the evening he attended a teachers' conference.

Early the next morning he posted an essay he had written to Albert Steffen and then went to the Waldorf School again. At 8 p.m. he gave a lecture for members (in CW 224) and then attended a meeting of the Group of 30. The 5th of July was devoted to discussions with the Waldorf School administration.

Those were the first five days of the month in detail. To continue with less detail, Rudolf Steiner worked in Dornach again from 6th to 10th July, went to Stuttgart again on the 11th to 14th, where among many other things he gave four lectures for Christian Community priests. Following his return to Dornach he attended eurythmy performances on 15th and 17th July. A lecture he gave there for members on 15th July has been published in CW 255.

The International Delegates Conference was held at the Goetheanum on 20th to 22nd July, and those were very full days. On the 23rd, Rudolf Steiner reviewed the plans for the coming Christmas Conference and the establishment of national societies with 26 of the delegates. He also had a meeting with German delegates on the 24th.

The first three lectures in this volume were given on the 27th to 29th July, and on the 30th of July he created the *St John's Imagination* pastel sketch. Then he went to Stuttgart again, to work with the teachers, returning to Dornach on the 31st.

Readers will be aware that Rudolf Steiner did at all times also have to respond to people who came to him with all kinds of concerns and requests.

He went to England via the Hook of Holland with Marie Steiner, arriving in Harwich where George Kaufmann (later Adams) came to meet them. They reached Ilkley in the evening of 4th August. The conference of the Educational Union for the Realization of Spiritual Values in Education, arranged by Margaret McMillan, was held in Ilkley. Rudolf Steiner and the teachers from Stuttgart who had come with him gave a course on the new method of education there. On 18th August they went from Ilkley to Penmaenmawr for the Summer School. He went to see the ancient Druid sites near Penmaenmawr, and the report he gave in Dornach on his visit to England is included in this volume.

Rudolf Steiner and his companions went on to London on 1st September 1923. They attended Society meetings there, Rudolf Steiner gave lectures for members, including the one printed in this volume, and for physicians. They visited Margaret McMillan's educational establishment in Deptford which made a deep impression. This clearly was a kindred spirit.

The travellers returned to Dornach on the 5th or 6th September, and Rudolf Steiner continued his work there, also giving the lecture on 10th September which is included in this volume. He went to Stuttgart again on 13th September. The last three lectures in this volume were given in Stuttgart.

Even in this greatly abbreviated form, the account of Rudolf Steiner's activities during those few months in 1923 is simply breathtaking, especially when we read his lectures and the report on his visit to England and consider the quality of the work.

As far as language is concerned, I have found it interesting to note that when speaking to members in Dornach and Stuttgart, people who we may assume were familiar with anthroposophy and with Rudolf Steiner's way of speaking, he would occasionally use an unusual turn of phrase. A verb would have a somewhat surprising object or subject, for instance. There we can really feel how he was endeavouring to put things into words for which the language did not really have the words. And in avoiding the usual he lifted the meaning out of the everyday rut. I have tried to match this in my translation into English. The interesting point is that Rudolf Steiner did not do this when speaking to the English. There he adhered to everyday usage. This shows a real regard for the needs and capabilities of a given audience, and perhaps also for his interpreter. It was not that George Adams would not have managed very well, but it could have been a problem for the audience.

Anna R. Meuss
Stroud, March 2016

Acknowledgement

I am greatly indebted to David E. Jones who has patiently gone through every text item, commenting and advising on some points and picking up the occasional typing errors which I had missed.
A.R.M.

Part One

THE SPIRITS INHABITING OUR PLANETARY SYSTEM

PLANETS WHICH DETERMINE DESTINY AND THOSE WHICH FREE HUMANITY

Lecture 1

During these days I would like to add to the things I said before,[1] and this will make it possible to gain insight into some of the background to the cosmic secrets that have been lost sight of in the civilization of more recent times. We merely have to look at the view taken of the planetary system, for instance, in more recent times. We know that this planetary system is thought to have arisen from a kind of nebula that was in rotation, with the individual planetary bodies splitting off from the nebula because of the rotation. The speculative ideas developed to suit this view have not given us anything but a kind of indifference among the individual heavenly bodies which I have described, and also indifference of the human eye in beholding these heavenly bodies.

What marked difference is there, we say, between moon and Saturn if it is all said to come from the idea of a rotating nebula from which they gradually split off? Yes, the research work done in the nineteenth century, which has been so significant for all things on earth and particularly the minerals on earth, has provided all kinds of detail about the chemical composition of the heavenly bodies, creating a kind of physics and chemistry for those bodies. As a result it is, of course, possible for the usual handbooks to provide particular details about Venus, Saturn, the moon and so on. But it is just as if we were to produce a kind of image of the external organism of the human being—who is endowed with soul and spirit—and not give any thought to that soul and spirit.

We must find a way again to enter, with the help of an initiation science, into something which in the first place we may call the endowment of our planetary system with soul and spirit, though today I would simply wish to concentrate more on a characterization of the individual nature of the planets in this system.

Let me first of all refer to the planet which is closest to the earth. The destiny of the earth is—in one particular respect—connected with the destiny of this planet, and there was a time when it played a completely different role in the life of the earth from the one it plays today. You know from what it says in my *Occult Science, an Outline* that in relatively recent cosmic times this heavenly body, the moon, was still united with the earth; it then separated from it and now orbits it.

If we speak of it as though it were a physical body in the heavens, the physical part of it is merely the external, the most external revelation of the spiritual principle which is behind it. To those who are able to get to know it in its outer and its inner aspect, it first of all presents itself in our universe as a gathering of spirits who are very much complete in themselves. Seen from outside, the moon essentially acts like a mirror reflecting the universe.

[Starting to draw on the blackboard, see Fig. 1 see p. 14.] So if this is the earth, and we put the moon in close proximity to the earth, taking the most superficial view, the situation is that it reflects the light of the sun when it shows itself. We may say that what comes to us from the moon is sunlight that has shone upon it and is reflected back. In the first place, therefore, the moon is the mirror reflecting the light of the sun. As you know, it is in the nature of a mirror that you see something reflected that is outside it, in front of it, and definitely do not see anything that is behind it. But the moon is not only the mirror of sun nature in the universe, as it were, but altogether a mirror for everything that may shine upon it. It is just that the light of the sun is most powerful. Everything that exists as a cosmic body in the universe shines on the moon, and the moon acts like a mirror for the whole universe, reflecting the image of this universe in all directions. We are therefore able to say that when we look at the universe it appears to us twice over—the way in which it is revealed in the world around our earth, and the way in which the moon reflects it. The sun's rays are powerful. They are also powerful when reflected by the moon. Everything else in the universe that is able to reveal itself by shining out into space is also reflected by the moon, and apart from the universe as it reveals itself to us, we also have the reflection of the universe that is coming from the moon.

If anyone were able to observe the moon in every detail, or in other words had an eye for the mirror images of the universe which the moon casts in every direction, they would have the whole universe reflected by the moon. However, everything which exists inside the moon remains the moon's secret, if I may put it like this. It remains hidden just as anything that is behind a mirror remains hidden. Anything behind the moon's surface, that is, inside the moon itself, is above all significant in its spiritual aspect.

The spirits which inhabit this inner part of the moon close themselves off from the rest of the universe in the strictest sense of the word. They live as if in a moon fastness. One must be able to develop a relationship to the light of the sun, manage to develop certain qualities in the life of the human heart in such a way that one does not see the reflections cast by the moon. Then the moon will in a way become transparent to the soul and one will be able to enter into this moon fastness in the universe. One will then make a significant discovery. One will find that certain secrets which the most select people on earth once knew but which have since been lost can be revealed again in what the spirits teach which have withdrawn, as it were, into total seclusion in this moon fastness in the universe.

Going back through earth evolution today we find that the further we go back the less do we come across the abstract truths which are people's pride and joy today. Instead we come more and more to truths which show themselves in the form of images. We then fight our way through the inwardly significant truths which still exist in written form, a last echo of oriental wisdom in the Vedas and

Vedanta,[2] for instance. We fight our way through to the original revelations made to humanity that are still behind myths and legends, and with great wonder and awe come to realize that human beings once had a magnificent wisdom given to them as a grace by the cosmic spirits, given in a way that required no effort on their part. And in the end we are taken back to everything those spirits had once been able to teach the early human beings who were then on earth. Now those spirits have withdrawn into the moon fastness of the universe, departing from the earth with the moon. Human beings retained a memory of what those spirits had once revealed to the earliest peoples of the human race who were still very different in their nature from the present-day human form.

Fathoming this secret—I'd like to call it the moon secret of the universe—you grow aware of the fact that the spirits which today have anchored themselves in the moon fastness of the universe once were the great teachers of humanity on earth, and that humanity on earth has lost the very thing in terms of spirit and soul which now lies hidden in that fastness in the universe. Anything which still comes to earth from the universe is very much limited to what the rest of the universe, the outer aspect—the walls, as it were—of that fastness, reflect back.

This moon secret is one of the most profound secrets of the ancient mysteries. For the moon holds 'original wisdom', as it were, within it. The reflection of the whole universe which the moon is able to produce creates the sum of powers that maintain the animal world on earth, especially the powers connected with sexuality in the animal world. These powers also maintain the physical animal nature of man and are connected with physical, sensual human sexuality. The lower nature of man is therefore a creation of the reflections coming from the moon, whereas the most sublime element which the earth once possessed now lies hidden inside the moon fastness.

Looking at the matter in this way we gradually come to know the moon's individual nature, know what it really is. All other knowledge is merely the kind of thing we would get of a person if we were to find a papier-mâché copy of him in a collection of curios. We would know nothing of his individual nature when looking at the papier-mâché figure. In the same way a science where people are not prepared to consider initiation cannot tell them anything about the individual nature of the moon.

In a sense the outermost planet—outermost at least for the ancients; Uranus and Neptune were discovered later on, and we won't give them our consideration just now—is the opposite to the moon in its individual nature. This is Saturn in its individual nature [green in Fig. 1]. Its nature is such that whilst it is stimulated by the universe itself in many different ways, it does not allow any of those stimuli from the universe to go back to the earth, does not reflect them for the earth. Yes, the sun also shines on Saturn, but any reflection Saturn produces of the sun's rays has no significance for life on earth. Saturn simply is the cosmic body in our planetary system which gives itself up wholly, in all it is. It lets its own essential nature shine out into the world. When we look at Saturn, it is really always telling us what it is by nature. When we look at the moon in its outer aspect, it tells us about everything else in the world. Saturn does not tell us anything about the stimuli it receives from the rest of the world but always speaks only of itself. It will only tell us about itself. And it gradually becomes apparent that Saturn is something like a kind of memory in our planetary system.

Saturn seems to us like the cosmic body which has faithfully taken part in everything in our planetary system and has also faithfully remembered it all in this cosmic remembrance. Saturn says nothing about present-day things in the universe. It takes them in, and works through them in its inner soul and spirit. The sum of the spirits that dwell in Saturn does give itself up to the outside world, but takes in the events in the world, takes them into its soul in complete silence, speaking only of past events in the cosmos. When first considered in cosmic terms, Saturn is therefore something like the perambulating memory in our planetary system. Faithfully imparting what has happened in the planetary system it really does in this way hold the secrets of the planetary system within it.

So we look in vain to the moon when we want to fathom the

secrets of the world, but have to become intimate with the spirits that dwell on the moon, as it were, in order to learn something about the world's secrets from them. This is not necessary in the case of Saturn. With Saturn, all it needs is to be open for things of the spirit. Then Saturn changes into a living historiographer for the planetary system before the eye of the spirit, the inner eye. It does not even hold back with the stories it can tell of everything that has been happening within the planetary system. In this respect it is the exact opposite of moon nature; it is talking all the time. And it speaks of the planetary system's past with inner warmth, an inner glow, which means that it is actually dangerous to be intimately acquainted with anything which Saturn says in the universe, for it speaks of past events in the universe with such devotion that one develops a tremendous love for this past of the universe. Saturn is, as it were, always tempting those who listen intently to learn its secrets to set little store by earthly things and enter fully and wholly into the past, into what earth has once been.

Saturn above all speaks clearly about everything the earth was before it came to be earth. It is therefore the one planet in our system which makes the past infinitely dear to us. And it is people who always like to look into the past, not liking progress but always wanting to bring back the past who have an earthly liking for Saturn. This is the way in which we come closer to the individual nature of Saturn.

A planet like Jupiter, for example [yellow in Fig. 1], is different by nature again. Jupiter is the thinker in our planetary system, and thinking is above all the element enjoyed by all the spirits which may be said to be united in Jupiter's cosmic terrain. Creative and received thoughts of the universe shine out to us from Jupiter. This planet holds all the powers to create the different spirits in the universe, doing so in thought form. Saturn speaks of the past; Jupiter shows what corresponds to it in the present of the universe but does so in a presentation that is alive, in a living way. We must, however, use what Jupiter presents to the inner eye in the right and proper way. If we do not develop our own thinking we will not even gain access to its secrets as clairvoyants, if I may use the word. The nature of Jupiter's secrets is such that they reveal themselves only in the form of thoughts, and we will only gain access to Jupiter's secrets if we do our own thinking, seeing that Jupiter is the thinker in the universe.

When you try to get a clear idea about some important riddle of existence and find you cannot do so because of the obstacles presented by the human physical and etheric and above all the astral obstacles, the Jupiter spirits will come in to help. The Jupiter spirits are indeed coming to help us to develop human wisdom. When someone has made a real effort to think clearly about some riddle of existence and cannot get to the bottom of it, he will find that if he is patient and continues to occupy himself with the riddle in his mind the powers from Jupiter will even come to help during the night. If someone who has found a better solution to a day's problem during the night, seemingly in his dreams, and were able to know the truth of this, he'll really have to admit: It is the Jupiter spirits who bring movement, swing and verve into human thinking (if I may put it like this). Human beings owe everything they have by way of the spiritual present of the universe to Jupiter. They owe everything they have by way of the past in spirit and soul to Saturn.

The ancient Greeks, who lived so much in the present, had some intuition that made them specially venerate Jupiter.

Jupiter also lends something to the successive seasons which provides a stimulus for human beings in the whole of their development. You know that if we look at the apparent movement of Saturn it moves very, very slowly, needing almost 30 years. Jupiter orbits more quickly, needing about 12 years. With this faster movement it exactly satisfies the human need for wisdom. And if according to the clock which may be said to reflect human destiny in the universe there is a special relationship between Jupiter and Saturn, then those marvellous and glorious, luminous moments enter into this human destiny when the thinking of the present reveals many things about the past.

When we look for the moments in humanity's world history when renaissance periods came and earlier impulses arose again, as for instance in the last Renaissance period, this renewal of earlier impulses is certainly connected with Jupiter and Saturn being in a particular relative position.

However, as I said, in a sense Jupiter is certainly a closed book, and its revelations remain at the unconscious level unless people meet it with active, clear thinking, strong in itself and full of light. In earlier times, when active thinking had not far developed, the way in which humanity progressed did really always depend on the relative positions of Jupiter and Saturn. Much would be revealed to people in earlier times when Jupiter and Saturn were in particular relative positions. People of more recent times have to depend more on taking things separately as they develop, that is, to receive Saturn memory and Jupiter wisdom separately as they develop in soul and spirit.

Let us move on to Mars [orange in Fig. 1]. Mars is the planet which we might call the talkative planet (you know how it is, we have to have a terminology). Mars does not, like Jupiter, hold back with its wisdom in the form of thoughts but is really always spilling the beans about everything accessible to it in the universe—not all things in the universe are accessible to it or rather the souls which dwell on it. It is the most gossipy planet in our planetary system, always talking. Mars is taking particular effect, for instance, when people talk in their sleep, in their dreams. For essentially it is the planet that has a tremendous desire to keep talking. If there is anything in human nature open to it so that it can make it rattle on, Mars will turn people into chatterboxes. It is the planet which thinks little, has few thinkers but many talkers. Its spirits are always on the lookout as to what shows itself here and there in the universe, and they will then talk about it with great interest and great verve. In the course of human evolution, Mars encourages people to talk about the secrets of the universe. It has its positive and its negative side. It has genius and also its demon. The genius brings it about that people actually get the impulses for speech and language from the universe. Its demon brings it about that speech and language are abused in many different ways. It may be called the 'agitator' in the universe—

there is a sense in which this is true. Mars wants to persuade, whereas Jupiter only wants to convince.

Venus, for instance, takes yet another position [violet in Fig. 1]. In some respect—now how can I put this?—Venus is stand-offish with regard to the whole universe. She is withdrawn, does not want to know of the universe. The attitude of Venus towards the universe is that if she were to open up to it she would, exactly because of the outer universe, lose her virginity. Venus is absolutely shocked when any kind of impression seeks to come to her from the outer universe. This planet does not like the universe, rejects every dancer coming from the outer universe. It is difficult to put this in words because we have to use earthly language, but that is how it is. On the other hand Venus is tremendously receptive to anything which comes from the earth. In a sense the earth is Venus' lover. The moon reflects the whole universe all round; Venus reflects nothing of the universe, does not want to know about anything which has to do with the universe, but lovingly reflects everything that comes to her from the earth. Spying on the secrets of Venus with the inner eye you get the whole earth again with all its secrets of the soul.

It is indeed the case that essentially people on earth cannot secretly do anything real in their souls without it being a reflection coming down from Venus, something we discover if we go into the matter. Venus looks deeply into human hearts, for this is of interest to her, it is something she does allow to reach her. Everything which lives in the inmost heart on earth is also found on Venus thanks to a mirroring of an unusual kind. Venus is really transforming everything as it is reflected just as dreams transform the external events of physical life. Venus takes the events on earth and changes them into dream images. The whole orbit in which Venus moves around the earth, this whole Venus sphere, is really a dream state. The secrets of human beings on earth are transformed as in a dream and live there in many different dream forms. Venus actually has a great deal to do with the poets. The poets themselves do not know this, of course, but Venus has a great deal to do with them.

But the whole thing is very strange. I said that Venus is stand-offish against the rest of the universe, and that is indeed the case. But she is not equally stand-offish against everything coming from the universe. I would say that in heart and mind Venus rejects everything coming from the universe except for anything coming from the earth. She rejects every dancer, I said, but she listens most attentively to everything which Mars is saying. Venus transforms, bringing light into her dreamlike earthly experiences with everything which Mars passes on to her from the universe.

There is also a physical side to all such things. The impulses arise from them for everything that is done in the world, comes about in the world. And Venus takes in everything that comes from the earth and is always listening in on Mars. She does not want Mars to know this but she wants to listen in. Out of all this—the sun is also there, establishing order—develop the powers that are the very basis for the human organs of speech.

If we want to know the impulses for human speech development in the cosmos, we must consider the to and fro, all the activity that goes on between Venus and Mars. The relative positions of Venus and Mars therefore have great significance for the way in which the language of a nation develops according to the twists and turns of destiny. A language gains in inner depth, in soul, when Venus happens to be in quadrature with Mars. On the other hand a language grows soulless, tinkling, when Venus and Mars are in conjunction, and this has an influence on the nation concerned.[3]

That is how these impulses which are developing in the universe appear to us which then also influence life on earth.

Now here we have Mercury [blue in Fig. 1]. Mercury is the planet which, unlike the others, is really interested in anything which is not sense perceptible by nature but so that one can make combinations with it. In Mars we have the masters of making combinations in thinking, in Jupiter the masters of wisdom-filled thinking. When human beings come from pre-earthly life into earthly existence it is the moon impulse which provides the powers needed for physical existence. Venus provides the powers for all qualities of mind and temperament. Mercury, on the other hand, provides the powers for the qualities of our rational understanding. The masters of powers of insight gained by making combinations are anchored in Mercury.

Once again there is a strange relationship among these planets where the human being is concerned. The moon, with the austere spirits in it that are wholly withdrawn into themselves, merely reflecting anything shining out to it from the universe, really builds up the external part, the body of the human being. In thus building up the bodily aspect it brings together the forces of heredity. The spirits in the moon have closed themselves off completely as they reflect, cosmically I would say, on anything which goes on from generation to generation via the physical aspect.

It is because the moon spirits are thus holed up in their fastness that nothing is known at all about heredity in modern science. Essentially it seems, if one takes a deeper look, that when people talk of heredity somewhere in a scientific context, then, speaking in cosmic terms, we might well say: 'That man is moon-abandoned; on the other hand he is Mars-bewitched for he is under the influence of the demonic Mars powers in talking about heredity, and he is far, far away from the actual secrets of heredity.'

Venus and Mercury are more bringing the soul and spirit of the karmic element into human beings, letting it show itself in their state of mind and temperament. Mars, and above all Jupiter and Saturn, have a liberating quality if people relate to them in the right way. They tear human beings away from anything which is determined by destiny and downright make them into free individuals.

We might almost use biblical terms to say, in a slightly changed form, 'Saturn, the faithful keeper of memories in the universe, said one day: Let us make man free in his own memory. The influence of Saturn was then pushed down into the unconscious, man developed his own memory and with this the foundation, the pledge, for his freedom as an individual.'

And the inner will impulse in our free thinking is a grace given by Jupiter. Jupiter could indeed control all human thoughts. It is the planet where we find the present thoughts of the whole universe if we

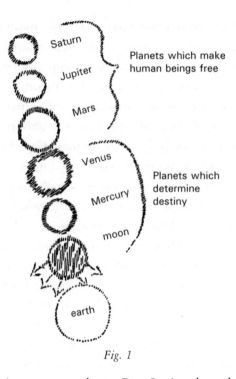

Fig. 1

are able to gain access to them. But Jupiter has also withdrawn, letting human beings be free in their thinking.

The element of freedom we have in speech consists in that even Mars has grown gracious. Because Mars has to accept, as it were, the decision of the other outer planets, and is not permitted to go on imposing things on human beings, man is in a way also free in his speech—not entirely so, but he is free in a way.

Seen from a different point of view, Mars, Jupiter and Saturn may therefore be called the planets that make human beings free, whereas Venus, Mercury and moon must be called the planets that determine destiny [Fig. 1].

The sun then takes its position among these actions and impulses of individual planets, creating harmony, as it were, between those which make man free and those which determine destiny. The sun is therefore the individual spirit where destiny-determining necessity and freedom-making principles come together in a truly marvellous way. One will only understand what the leaping, blazing light of the sun contains if one thus sees the interweaving life and activity of destiny and freedom in this light which spreads out into the world and then again keeps warmly together in the sun.

We also do not manage very well with the sun itself if we limit ourselves to what physicists know of it. We will only manage with the sun if we look to the soul and spirit of it. There the sun is the principle that makes necessity of destiny come aglow in warmth, and resolves destiny into freedom in the flame, and when freedom is misused the sun gathers it together in its effective substantial aspect. The sun is the flame, as it were, in which freedom shows itself phosphorus-like in the universe. At the same time it is the substance in which, like in ashes that agglomerate, the misused freedom coheres, as destiny, so that it may continue to be active until this destiny in its turn can phosphorus-like change into the flame of freedom.

Lecture 2

YESTERDAY I spoke of the starry heavens closest to us. Thinking back on this you will above all have to say: When such a characterization of the starry heavens is gained through spiritual insight it is very different from anything that is generally said on the subject today. To make this clear I spoke in a particular way about it yesterday. I had to speak about it in a way which must seem absurd, even ridiculous, to anyone who learns about the subject in contemporary education today. Yet the situation is that our sick life in mind and spirit can only find a kind of healing if there can be this complete change in the way we look at things, especially those we were considering yesterday.

It seems fair to say that where thinking is done today, but in such a way that the thinking runs on the old, generally accepted rails, we see on the one hand that the thinking does everywhere point to this new form of spiritual insight. On the other hand we also see that people are not in a position to go along the route that leads to that kind of spiritual view. So they are really at a loss everywhere and—which is perhaps the worst part of it at the present point in time—are not aware of their helplessness, and indeed do not want to be aware of it.

Let us consider how the things I spoke of yesterday from a completely different point of view are described today. I spoke of moon, Saturn, Jupiter and so on and of the individual spirits which we may connect with those terms. In a way I presented our planetary system as a gathering of spirits which act on different impulses, but in such a way that these impulses also have something to do with the things that happen on earth. We saw living entities with distinct character appear in the universe. We were able to speak of spirits alive in Saturn, the moon, and so on. But the whole way in which one speaks is different from what is generally said about such things today. People assume—let me repeat this once more—that there was once a nebula and it was rotating. The individual planets, today regarded in complete indifference, more or less seen as luminous physical bodies rushing along in cosmic space, are said to have split off from the nebula.

This view, that the heavenly bodies are such unimportant bodies where all one can do is to use physics, and particularly mathematics, to calculate their orbits and possibly investigate if the forms of matter found on earth may also be found there, this indifferent way of looking at the heavenly bodies is something which has really only become customary in the last three or four hundred years. It has become customary in a particular way. It is simply that people do not realize this today. Since we have lost the possibility of seeing into the spiritual or, as was the only remaining possibility in medieval times, at least of having an inkling of it, it has become possible for us to lose the spiritual altogether. People then came to see the physical concepts which they had on earth, mathematical concepts, calculations, as something certain, and therefore also calculated the things that show themselves in the heavens. A particular precondition was established—I have to go a bit into these theoretical aspects today—that once people had learned how to calculate something on earth, developing the science of physics, they would apply that science also to the whole of the heavens, thinking that the results of calculations made on earth also applied in celestial space.

On earth we speak of time, of matter, of motion, and if we are physicists we might also refer to mass, velocity, and so on. All these are concepts gained on earth. Since Newton's day[4] this has been extended to cover celestial space. And the whole way in which people see what goes on in the cosmos is nothing but the result of calculations gained on earth and then flung out into the heavens. The whole of Kant-Laplace's nebular hypothesis[5] becomes an absurdity the moment we realize that it applies only on the assumption that the same laws of arithmetic apply out there in cosmic spaces as on earth, that the concepts of space, time, and so on apply out there just as much as on earth.

Now there is, however, a strange fact, a fact that makes people rack their brains. We are living in strange times, as evident in many symptoms. At all the popular meetings held by monists and other leagues[6] it is said to be a certainty that the stars are shining out there because of the well-known processes. A gullible public is presented by popular speakers and writers with the beautiful theory of spiral nebulas and so on which are apparent to the physical eye. And people get their education today from those popular speakers and writers. Essentially, however, this education is merely the result of things which physicists and other 'learned' people thought up decades ago. Things are rehashed at those popular gatherings which the experts considered to be true decades ago. Today something quite different is exciting the experts. Today it is the 'theory of relativity', for instance, which excites them.

This theory of relativity, Einstein's theory of relativity,[7] occupies the minds of the thinkers among physicists today. It is, of course, possible to speak about details of this theory the way I have been doing here and there; but today we will not consider its inner validity but the fact that it exists and that physicists talk about it. There are also physicists who oppose it, but very many physicists simply are speaking of the theory of relativity. Now what does this signify?

It signifies that this theory of relativity is destroying all the concepts that are behind the view of the movements and nature of the heavenly bodies in cosmic space. The things still told to lay people today in popular talks and books and written in works on astronomy were accepted as the truth for decades. But the physicists are busy in breaking down, destroying the most popular concepts—time, movement, space—and say that none of it truly is the way people thought it was. You see, for physicists at least it is now something like a matter of conscience to say, for instance: 'I direct my telescope towards a distant star. But I have worked out that so and so much time passes before the light from that star gets down to earth. When I look through my telescope, therefore, the light I see has needed so and so many light years to reach it. The light in my telescope was therefore emitted so and so many light years ago. The star is no longer in the place where I see it. The ray of light reaches my telescope, but the star is no longer in the place to which the telescope extends. When I look at a neighbouring star, the light of which needs far fewer light years, this light nevertheless gets here at the same time. I move the telescope. The star appears in a point of light which perhaps was there so and so many years ago. Now I move it again. A star appears in the telescope which actually is not there, but has been there a completely different number of years ago. And that is how I form ideas about my starry heavens. All of it has been there since it came to be there but in reality it is not there at all. In reality there is nothing there—everything has gone higgledy-piggledy.'

It is exactly the same with space. We hear a distant sound. The pitch changes as we come closer to it, different from when we move away from it. Space determines the nature of what we perceive. And that is, of course, a puzzle to people. Time, which enters into all our calculations, has suddenly become something quite uncertain, something which is merely relative. A modern physicist—who would, of course, be fully aware of this—can only say about everything which is pictured out in cosmic space in such a popular way: 'Something has been there once, is still there, will be there one day. Yes, well, there is something there. And whatever is there is responsible for the fact that at a certain point in time the light it emits coincides with the cross-wires in my telescope.' The only wisdom which still remains for us concerns the coincidences of two events. Something which has happened somewhere at some time coincides with what happens in the cross-wires of my telescope today. 'All we can speak of are such coincidences,' says the modern physicist, 'all of it is relative. The concepts that make up the theory of the world edifice are indeed only relative and have no absolute validity.' And if you were to leave a gathering of lay people today and go immediately to a lecture given by a relativity theoretician you would find that the popularizing speaker was handing something down to people based on ideas of which the experts would say: 'All that has melted away like snow in the sun.'

You see, it is not only that we can say that a physical view of the world has evolved from certain concepts in the last 300 or 400 years. We also have to say that there are enough people today who in working with these concepts have reduced them to nothing, destroyed them. That view of the world, which people think is so certain, no longer exists for a great many thinkers today. So it is after all not really permissible to say that something said from a completely new point of view may be ridiculed. For the things said from that other point of view are presently melting away like the snow in the sun. For those who know about these things, or at least want to know something about them, they are actually no longer there. The fact is, therefore, that people say, 'The things described here from the spiritual-scientific point of view are absurd, for they do not agree with the things we consider to be correct.' But speaking from the point of view of relativity these people then have to say: 'The things we thought were correct are absurd.' That is how things are today. The majority of people are really asleep and sleep as they watch these things taking their course; they let them happen. But it is important to know that the view of the world which as such has been so triumphant really lies all in ruins today.

The true situation in the spiritual world will really only be clearly understood more widely when people raise the nightcap they are wearing at least a little bit. So it is certainly possible to think that something which speaks in the kind of tenor in which I spoke yesterday is absurd in the face of modern science, for in its theory of relativity, for instance, this science is wholly negative. It is really always telling us what is *not*, and humanity will need to steer towards insight into what *is*.

These things have to be done with the kind of presentation I tried to make yesterday, speaking of individual stars in our planetary system. But what do we see there? We see that in a sense, people follow the course of world evolution with great accuracy. What would an old-fashioned physicist—not a new-fashioned one, for they are mostly relativity theoreticians—say if he were to hear one say something as outrageous as I did yesterday? If he did not immediately say that all of it is rubbish and quite wrong, and that might well be what he'd say at first, he would certainly insist that it goes against the solid foundations of science. Yet what are the solid foundations of science? They are the concepts of space, time and so on which people have gained on earth. Now the relativity theoreticians destroy these concepts where the universe is concerned and declare them to have no validity.

In anthroposophy, on the other hand, the approach is practical. The earthly concepts are left aside when speaking of moon, Saturn, Jupiter and so on. There we do no longer speak of the earthly sphere but try—though it is not an easy thing to do—to characterize Venus and Mars in a way that cannot be done with earthly concepts. We have to agree to let go of the earthly concepts if we want to penetrate up into the universe. I wanted to show you how the cosmos has its position in present-day cultural life and how things actually are in the life of modern culture. Only one relationship with the earthly concepts remains when we go out into the cosmos. Just consider, if we go only as far as the moon, as I characterized it yesterday, to the spirits which are anchored in the moon as in a cosmic fastness and actually live behind the outer surface of the moon—where, if I may put it like this, they pursue their cosmic business—when we come to these spirits, which we can only do if clairvoyance sharpens our sight, we do find that they do their business in seclusion. Nothing which is inside the moon goes out into the world, and everything which does come from the moon has been cast back from the world. The moon does not take in the sunlight but reflects it, and it also reflects everything else that happens in the universe. Everything that happens in the universe is reflected by the moon as if in a mirror. The things that happen inside the moon remain hidden.

I did, however, say to you that the spirits which are holed up in this moon fastness and in the universe and pursue their cosmic business in there had once been on earth, before the moon split off from the earth. They had been the first great teachers of human souls on earth. The great, most ancient wisdom of which people speak is essentially a legacy from these moon spirits who today live hidden lives in the moon. They have withdrawn there.

When one speaks about the universe in this way, moral concepts enter into the ideas one is developing. We ask ourselves: 'Why did these moon spirits withdraw? Why do they do their work in hiding?' Yes, when they were still on earth they did indeed suggest a tremendous wisdom to human beings. If they had stayed on earth they would have been suggesting this wisdom all the time, but people would then never have been able to enter into the age of freedom.

Those spirits had made the wonderful decision, as it were, to withdraw from the earth, withdraw to a closed place in the universe. There they would pursue their cosmic business far removed from humanity so that human beings would not be influenced any further by them, so that human beings would be able to take in all the impulses of the universe and be free spirits. Those spirits chose a new dwelling place in the universe for themselves, so that freedom would gradually be possible for human beings.

Yes, that is talking in a different way from the way in which physicists talk. Hearing that the moon had split off from the earth, a physicist would simply calculate the speed at which this happened, the energies involved, and all of this always only with earthly energies, earthly velocities in mind. When we speak of the moon the way I did yesterday, those factors are simply ignored. Yet when we ignore the physical aspects, there remain those decisions, those great cosmic moral impulses. From going on about physics, which do apply to conditions on earth, we come to speak about the universe in moral ideas.

This is what matters, that one does not merely establish theories which people are meant to believe but the fact that there is a moral world order. Over the last three or four centuries the human soul has grown quite confused because people said that it is possible to know something about the earth and according to what is known about the earth calculate the universe and establish Kant-Laplace's nebular hypothesis and similar theories, but when it comes to the divine moral world order you have to *believe*. This has confused people enormously, because all realization has been lost that we must speak in earthly terms about the earth but the moment we ascend to the universe we must begin to speak in cosmic terms. There physical talk gradually becomes moral talk. There something is practised which otherwise is at best only invented fantasy.

When you see the way a physicist describes the sun today, you find it is some kind of gas sphere, steaming out there, and its eruptions are described as if they were eruptions on earth. Everything is projected out on to this cosmic body the way things happen on earth, and we then use the calculations we have learned to do here to calculate how a light ray passes the sun, or the like. But the calculations which apply here for earthly things cease to be valid when we get out there. Just as the intensity of light is inversely proportional to the square of the distance from the source, so do the laws cease to be valid out there in the universe. And we are only related to the universe in our moral nature. Rising above the physical to the moral as human beings, we do here on earth grow to be similar to the morality brought to realization out there in cosmic space.

We therefore have to say that anthroposophy is science to the utmost degree. Here demands are actually met. One is no longer speaking in earthly ideas, except for the moral ideas, and these are super-earthly even on earth. In anthroposophy one refers to such moral ideas when one rises up to the universe. This must be thoroughly taken into account. And it is from this point of view that we must find the concepts which we need to understand what cannot yet be understood here on earth.

You see, the spirits which are anchored in the moon only act, as I said, as if in a fastness. There they pursue their cosmic business. For everything that the moon gives to the world, to the earth, is reflected, mirrored. This situation has, however, only come about in the course of evolution. It was different in the past. When those spirits were still on the earth they acted on the soft, I'd say slimy form that the earth itself and all creation on it once had. And in both human beings and animals the development of the spinal column was connected with the actions of those spirits. The spinal column of human beings and animals is thus a legacy from very early times when the moon spirits were still connected with earthly existence. It can no longer arise today. The spinal column is a legacy, it can no longer develop anew today.

For four-footed animals the spirits fixed the spine in such a way that it remains in the horizontal. For human beings they made it to be such that it could come into the vertical. With the vertical spine human beings could then grow free for the universe and its influences at the moment when the moon spirits withdrew into their moon fastness.

And so we will gradually come to explain the earthly from the standpoint of the universe and altogether judge spiritual impulses in the right way even in earthly existence. The situation is that things have come into human heads which have actually only come up in the last three or four centuries, all of them merely because of the view that only things learned from physical events and the physical things on earth can be used to explain the whole of the universe. The whole universe has been made into a physical image of the earth. Now, however, people have come to realize: 'Something is coinciding with my cross-wires, but it was there in the past!' But the whole thing simply is not valid like this. When things are taken into account with regard to stars that are far enough away, a modern physicist can certainly say: 'The map that I am drawing is of something that does not exist. I draw two stars side by side. One of them a thousand years ago, let us say, the other six hundred years ago. They have never existed side by side the way I see the light rays coincide in the cross-wires.'

So it all melts away. It is not at all like that in reality. These concepts will not let us realize what is out there. You do calculation upon calculation. It is just like a spider spinning its web and then imagining that this web goes through the whole world.

The reason is that the laws on which we base our calculations do not apply at all out there. At most we can use the moral quality in us to gain concepts of what exists out there. Out there in the starry heavens things go morally, sometimes also immorally, ahrimanically, luciferically and so on. But if I take 'moral' as a generic term, it is moral out there and not physical. This is something people will have to come to realize again, for over the last two or three centuries the other view has fixed itself so firmly in human heads that even the doubts that come to the minds of relativity theoreticians—there's a great deal to be said for their negations—cannot drive it out of their heads. And we can understand this, for when even this last phantom, the time and space calculation they do, when this also vanishes from people's heads when it comes to the starry heavens, nothing will be left in those heads, and people do like to have something in their heads. Something else can only be in there when people rise to the possibility of looking at the starry heavens in the way in which we did yesterday.

We have to realize that all this indicates how necessary it is for people today to gain clear ideas as to what really happened in the last three or four centuries, with the outcome so far the greatest of all wars ever known on earth and the chaotic conditions which will grow more and more chaotic in the near future. The demand humanity must face is that they do really get a clear idea of these things. And in this respect it is interesting to cast an eye on the earth and cultural development on earth today.

In the civilization in which westerners, including their American offshoot, live, people do simply consider that everything which has developed in the last three or four centuries under the influence of a phenomenally magnificent technology and magnificent transport and communications—which is also breaking down today—is so firmly established that anyone who does not think so must of course be a fool. It is true that the old culture of the Orient has gone into decline, but one must also say that the things which have to be said today, arising from the source springs of our own anthroposophical investigations, the way I said them yesterday, have in a far distant past been oriental wisdom, though of a very different kind.

As I have said on many occasions, we cannot accept this oriental wisdom in the old form today. We have to regain it from within western hearts and minds, from the western soul. But I would like to say that there was a time when it was the custom to speak about the stars in the way in which I started to speak of them again yesterday but out of the ancient clairvoyance, that dreamlike ancient clairvoyance. This is something humanity has lost altogether, and modern Europeans consider everything that once was seen as the most sublime human wisdom to be absurd.

Well, as I said, it may once have been a magnificent original wisdom yonder in the Orient, but today the ancient culture of those people has gone into decline. Yet in a sense something still survives, at least superficially, as tradition in the Orient, a way of looking at the universe that has soul, I'd say. And the Orientals are not very impressed by Europe's technological culture. The very souls which today give loving consideration to the original wisdom in the Orient are essentially despising the mechanical culture and civilization which has evolved in Europe. They study the ancient writings to consider the human soul. This gives some of them an inner enlightenment, though subject to decline, so that something still survives in the Orient of seeing the world with the eyes of the soul. And it is not in vain also to consider the way in which these people who have at least still some echo of an ancient culture consider the cultural life in Europe and America. It may just be for comparison but is interesting nevertheless.

A strange book has appeared by a gentleman called Ramanathan,[8] an Indian from Ceylon, *The Culture of the Soul among Western Nationals*. He puts things in a strange way. He evidently is someone in the Orient, in Indian civilization, who has said to himself: 'These Europeans do also have very strange writings, such as the New Testament.' Ramanathan and others have studied the New Testament but this was of course done in the way in which their souls enabled them to study it. They took in the New Testament, the things done by Christ Jesus, according to their state of soul. And one can see from Ramanathan's book that there are people in the Orient who speak of Christ Jesus and the New Testament out of what remains of their most ancient culture. They have developed their own, quite definite ideas of Christ Jesus.

Ramanathan has written a great deal about these ideas which he has of Christ Jesus, and he wrote the book—in English—for European readers. The book, written in the Indian spirit about Jesus in the Gospels is therefore addressed to the Europeans, and is telling them something very strange. He writes that it was really quite peculiar that they did not know anything at all about Christ Jesus. Magnificent things were written about Christ Jesus in the Gospels, he says, but the Europeans and Americans had no idea, truly no idea at all! He gives a peculiar piece of advice to the Europeans and Americans, asking them to accept teachers of the New Testament from India. They would be able to tell them the true situation concerning Christ Jesus.

The people over yonder in Asia who are today concerning themselves with progress in Europe and then read the New Testament are therefore telling Europeans: 'If you want to learn something about Christ Jesus, you have to accept teachers from India, for none of the teachers who are talking to you now have any idea at all. Everything they say comes from failure to understand!' Ramanathan goes into detail about this. He says that at a particular time in Europe, a way of understanding everything in words took the place of grasping the spiritual essence. Europeans depend on the understanding of words, in a way. They have no spiritual insight in their heads but the words which they learn in their individual nations rise like vapour up into their heads and they then think in words.

It is strange how the Indians gain this insight in spite of the decline in their ancient culture, for what they say is strikingly true up to this point. People think in words and not objects or situations today. People are really rather odd in this respect. Someone who wants to be taken to be really clever will quickly quote: 'For when concepts are lacking a word will soon come up.'[9] Today this happens mostly when the person concerned has no concepts at all. Then Goethe's words will soon come to mind. But the person does not realize this. He does not know that he himself is desperately caught up in the self-same failing even as he criticizes it.

So this Indian is saying to the Europeans: 'You only understand things in words and you have applied this understanding in words to the New Testament and therefore made the Christ dead for four hundred years. He is no longer living among you—he's been dead for four centuries. Find teachers from India for yourselves so that he may be brought to life again.' This is what this Indian is telling the Europeans.

He is saying that for three or four centuries the Europeans have simply known nothing at all about the Christ. They cannot know anything because they do not have the concepts and ideas which make it possible to know anything about the Christ. The Indian is telling the Europeans: 'You need a renaissance of Christ Jesus. You have to rediscover the Christ, or someone else has to discover him for you, so that you will have him again.' This is what the Indian is saying since he has read the Gospels himself. He realizes, therefore, that strange things have been going on in Europe for the last three or four centuries. And he then says that if the Europeans wanted to realize for themselves again the Christ who lives in the New Testament they would have to go a long way back. For this failure to understand the Christ has evolved slowly, and if the Europeans wanted to learn to understand anything about the Christ from their own documents they would need to go all the way back to Gnosis.

A strange phenomenon! There you have an Indian, merely representative of many, who reads the New Testament and tells Europeans: 'There is absolutely no help for you unless you go back to the Gnostics.'

But the Europeans really only have the Gnostics in the writings of their opponents. They do not know anything about the Gnostics. It is a strange fact that the writings of the Gnostics have all been eradicated, and all we have are the polemics of the Church Fathers against the Gnostics, the exception being the *Pistis Sophia*[10] and a few other documents. The way these are, however, they can be as little understood as the Gospels can be.

Now if one is not a Gnostic but finds the Christ again thanks to modern spiritual science, the theologians come and say: 'This is a rehash of Gnosis'—though they do not really know Gnosis, being quite unable to know it on the basis of some external things or others. But, they say, 'it is not permissible to rehash Gnosis, for Christianity is falsified in Gnosis'. Here we have a divergence between East and West. Someone studying the New Testament in the East finds that one needs to go back to the early centuries. When theologians of today think that the view taken of the Christ in present-day anthroposophy looks as if it is reminiscent of the Gnosis which they do not know, they will say: 'He wants to rehash Gnosis and that must not be, for it falsifies Christianity.' The Indian's view does indeed sound strange. Ramanathan is really saying that Christianity as Europeans see it today has been falsified. The Europeans say that Ramanathan is falsifying our Christianity. It is, however, Ramanathan who comes fairly close to the right view, though his way of looking at it comes from a culture in decline. Something which is right is always a falsification of what is false. We just have to call a spade a spade. The true is always a falsification of the false, for one would not arrive at the true if one did not falsify the false.

So that is how things are today. Just consider the abyss which opens up before us when we take this example of Ramanathan. Someone might, for instance, say: 'Read the Gospels without bias.' It is difficult for Europeans to read them without bias today. On the one hand they had to depend on the maltreated translations for centuries, and they have been brought up to have certain ideas. It is difficult to read them without bias. Yet when someone reads them without bias, even if from his particular point of view, he will find a spiritual Christ in the Gospels. Ramanathan discovered that spiritual Christ in the Gospels, though he is not yet able to see him in the anthroposophical sense. But the Europeans should at least take note that this Indian from Ceylon is advising them to have preachers about the Christ come from India, seeing that they do not have any.

With things like these we must have the courage today to look into developments over the last three or four centuries. It needs this courage to get out of the tremendous chaos into which humanity has been gradually getting itself. This tendency to be unclear clouds all concepts and ultimately also brings social chaos. For the things that go on between people do after all come from their souls, and there certainly is a connection between the most sublime truths and the destruction of external economic conditions. We must accept that we have to let go of earthly concepts if we want to rise to the universe.

In yesterday's lecture I sought to give you an example of how the cosmos relates to life in the spirit today and how things are in that life in the spirit. A kinship with earthly concepts exists only when we get out into the cosmos.

LECTURE 3

DORNACH, 29 JULY 1923[11]

THE levels of human conscious awareness, which we have been considering from several points of view in these days, vary during existence on earth between being fully awake, being asleep, and the dream state. In the short course of lectures I gave during the delegate conference[12] I did attempt to show the whole significance of dreaming. Today let us first of all consider the question 'Is it part of the essential nature of human beings to live in these three states of consciousness here on earth?'

We need to understand that only human beings live in these three states of conscious awareness during existence on earth. Animals live in a very different alternation. They do not have the deep dreamless sleep which human beings have for most of the time between going to sleep and waking up. Nor do they have the full waking consciousness which human beings have between waking up and going to sleep. The waking state of animals is really somewhat similar to human dreaming, though the conscious experiences of higher animals are more definite, richer, I'd say, than the passing dreams which human beings have. On the other hand animals are never in the state of high-degree unconsciousness in which human beings are in deep sleep.

Animals therefore are not as distinct from their environment as are human beings. They do not have an outside world and inner world the way human beings do. To put in human words what lives as a dim awareness in higher animals is that animals really see themselves and all their inner nature as part of the outside world.

When an animal sees a plant, it does not initially have the feeling that there is a plant out there and I am inwardly complete in myself. No, the animal has a powerful inner experience of the plant, a sympathy or antipathy that comes to immediate expression. The animal is, as it were, inwardly sentient of what the plant is saying. At the present time people are so little able to observe anything that does not present itself in quite a gross way. This prevents them from simply seeing from what animals do, from their behaviour, that it truly is exactly as I have said.

Only human beings have this power of making clear, definite distinction between their inner world and the outside world. Why do human beings accept that there is an outside world? What makes them speak at all of an inner world and an outside world? They do so because they are always out of their physical and ether body with their I and astral body when asleep, leaving their physical and ether body to themselves, as it were, in sleep, and are with the things that are outside world. In our sleep state we share the destiny of outside things. Tables and benches, trees and clouds are outside our physical and ether body in our waking state and we therefore refer to them as outside world. In sleep our own astral body and our own I are part of the outside world. And something happens whilst we belong to the outside world with our I and astral body in sleep.

To realize what is happening there, let us start with what is actually happening when we face the world in a wholly normal waking state. Physical objects are outside us. And scientific thinking has finally reached a point where only things that we can measure, weigh and count in the physical outside world are considered to be certain. The subject matter of our physical science is determined according to weight, measure and number.

We use the methods of calculation which apply to things on earth, we weigh things and measure them. Anything we assess according to weight, measure and number makes up the physical world. We would not call a body physical if we were unable to demonstrate its reality in some way using the scales. However, such things as colours, sounds, even sensations of heat or cold, i.e. the actual sensory perceptions, are somehow wafting across the things which have mass, measure and number. When we want to identify any physical object, its actual physical nature is indeed whatever can be weighed and counted, and that is really the only thing physicists want to concern themselves with. When it comes to colour, sound, and so on, they'll say: 'Well, something is going on outside which also has to do with weighing or counting.' With regard to colour phenomena they say: 'Out there are wave motions which make an impression on human beings, and when the eye establishes this impression they call it colour, and when the ear establishes it they call it sound, and so on.' We might actually say that modern physicists do not know what to do with all these things—sound, colour, heat and cold. They consider them to be properties of things that can be identified using scales, a measuring rod or calculation. The colours are in a way attached to the physical, sound wrests itself from the physical, heat or cold well forth from the physical. They say that something which has weight *has* redness, or *is* red.

When human beings are in the state between going to sleep and waking up, these things are different for the I and the astral body. First of all, the objects determined by measure, number and weight simply are not there. It may seem strange but when we are asleep we do not have things around us that can be weighed, nor things one is able to count or measure in a direct way. When we are I and astral body in sleep we would not be able to use a measuring rod. What we have there are, if I may put it like this, the free floating and moving sensory perceptions. However, at the present stage of evolution human beings are unable to perceive free floating redness, freely moving sound waves, and so on.

To make a diagram of this, we'd do something like this. We might say that here on earth we have things that are solid and can be weighed, and redness, yellowness is in a way attached to these weighable solid objects, being what the senses perceive in those objects. When we are asleep the yellowness is free floating quality,

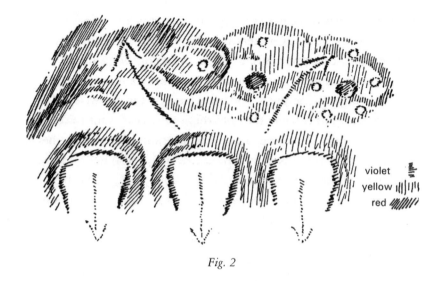

violet
yellow
red

Fig. 2

the redness is free floating quality, not attached to such conditions of gravity but floating and moving freely. It is the same with sound. It is not that the bell sounds, but the sound is actively moving [Fig. 2].

And you know, when we walk around in our physical world and see something, we pick it up; it is only then that it is truly an object, for otherwise it might also be something which deceives the eye. There must also be weight. This is why people are so inclined to consider something which appears in the physical world but does not have weight for them—the colours of the rainbow, for instance—to be an optical delusion. If you open a textbook on physics today you will find that it says this is merely an optical illusion. A raindrop is considered to be truly real. And people draw in lines which really have no significance for what is there, but which are thought to go through space; they are then called 'rays'. But those rays actually are not there. People then say that the eye projects this outward for itself. This business of projection is altogether something which is applied in a most peculiar way in modern physics. So I get the idea: 'We see a red object. To convince ourselves that it is not an optical illusion we pick it up and it is heavy. This confirms that it is real.'

Someone who comes to awareness in the I and astral body outside the physical and ether bodies will finally realize that there certainly is something of that kind in this colour or sound quality which floats and moves so freely. In a colour quality which thus floats freely lies the tendency to go out into far distant parts of the world; gravity is the opposite of this. These things on earth want to go down to the centre of the earth [Fig. 2, arrows going down]; those [arrows pointing upwards] want to move freely out into cosmic space.

There is also something there which is like a kind of measure. You'll discover this if there is a small reddish cloud somewhere, let us say, [Fig. 3] and this is hemmed with, let us say, a mighty yellow form. You then measure, not with a measuring rod, but qualitatively, using the red, which is the stronger colour, to gauge the fainter yellow. And where a measuring rod would tell you that you have five metres, the red will here tell you: 'If I were to spread, I'd fit five times into the yellow. I have to expand, grow in size, and then I'll also be yellow.' That is the way of measuring here.

It is even more difficult to get a clear idea about counting in this case because when we count things on earth we usually have just pears or apples lying side by side and indifferent to one another. And when we go from one to two we always have the feeling that the number one really is quite indifferent to the fact that there is also a number two beside it. This is different even in human life; there it is sometimes the case that number one has to depend on number two. And that does always take us into something non-physical. With actual physical mathematics the units[*] are always indifferent about anything that joins them. That is not the case here.

Fig. 3

---

[*] Earlier German editions had 'subdivisions'.

If we have one of a particular kind somewhere here, it calls for some, let us say three or five more, depending on how it is [Fig. 2, dots and small circles in red]. There is always an inner connection with the others and the number is something real. When there begins to be conscious awareness about how it is when one is out there with one's I and astral body, one will also come to establish something like measure, number and weight, but of the opposite kind.

Once seeing and hearing out there is no longer a mere wishy-washiness of red and yellow and sounds but we begin even there to be sentient of things having an order, we begin to perceive the spirits who bring themselves to realization in these free floating sensory perceptions. We then enter into the positive spiritual world, into the life and activities of the spirits. Here on earth we enter into the life and activities of earthly things by weighing, measuring and counting them. Learning the opposite to being heavy in a qualitative way, that is, seeking to expand easily, lightly into cosmic space, measuring colour with colour, and so on, we begin to grasp the nature of the spirits. Such spirits are also present throughout everything out there in the natural worlds.

In the waking state of mind we human beings see only the outer aspects of minerals, plants and animals. But in sleep we are with the spiritual element which lives in all these entities in the natural worlds. When we return to ourselves as we wake up, the I and astral body do in a way retain the inclination towards, the affinity with the objects outside, making us accept the reality of an outside world. If we had an organization that was not made for sleep we would not accept the fact of an outside world. It is not a question of someone suffering from insomnia, of course. For I am not saying 'when people do not sleep' but 'if we had an organization that was not made for sleep'. It is a matter of being prepared for something. This is also why people get sick when suffering from insomnia, for that is not in accord with their nature. But the way things are is that exactly because people dwell with their outside world in sleep, with the world which on waking they call their outside world, they also arrive at an outside world, a view of the outside world.

This relationship which people have to sleep provides the earthly concept of truth. In how far? Well, we call it truth when we are able to recreate the image of something outside within us, when we have a real living experience of something from outside within us. For this we need the institution of sleep. We would have no concept of truth if we did not have the institution of sleep. We are therefore able to say that we owe the truth to the sleep state. To give ourselves up to the truth of things we must also spend some of our time with them. The objects only tell us something about themselves because in our souls we are with them in sleep.

It is different for the dream state. As I told you in the short course of lectures during the delegate conference, the dream is related to memory, to the inner life, to the quality that lives above all in memory. When the dream is a free floating world of sound and colour we are still halfway out of our body. When we enter in completely, the powers that we unfold in a living, active way in our dream turn into powers of memory. We are then no longer distinct from the outside world. Our inner life comes together with the outside world and we live so powerfully in the outside world with our sympathies and antipathies that we are not sentient of those things as sympathetic or antipathetic but that the sympathies and antipathies themselves assume image nature.

If it were not possible for us to dream, with this dream power continuing on in our inner life, we would not have beauty. The fact that we actually have potential for beauty is due to our ability to dream. In everyday life we have to say that we owe it to dream power that we have a memory; when it comes to art in human life we owe beauty to the power of dream. The dream state is thus connected with beauty. For the way in which we are sentient of something being beautiful and create something that is beautiful is very close to the active, mobile power of dreaming.

When we experience beauty or create something beautiful— though we need our physical body to do so—we are behaving in a way which is similar to the way in which we behave when out of our physical body, or half connected with our physical body, when we dream. It is just a short step really, a tiny shift, from dreaming to living in beauty. And it is just that people are so gross in the materialistic age we live in that they do not notice this tiny shift, and they have so little awareness of the whole significance of beauty. One must of necessity give oneself up to it in one's dreams in order to experience this free floating and active life. If you give yourself to freedom, to inner arbitrariness, that is, if you live after the shift, you will no longer be sentient of it being the same as dreaming, for it is the same only when one uses the powers of the physical body.

People today will go on for a long time thinking about what one meant by saying 'chaos' in earlier times. The term is defined in many different ways. But the only true way of characterizing the term chaos is to say: When human beings enter into a state of conscious awareness where the experience of weight, an earthly measure, has just come to an end and things begin to be only half that weight yet do not yet want to go out into the universe but remain in the horizontal, in balance, when solid boundaries begin to wave, so that the indefinite aspect of the world is seen still with the physical body but already with the mental constitution of dreaming, that is when we see chaos. And the dream is but chaos floating towards the human being like a shadow.

In ancient Greece people were still sentient of the fact that we cannot really make the physical world beautiful. The physical world is necessarily natural; it is as it is. We can only create beauty from chaos. Beauty arises when we transform chaos into cosmos. Chaos and cosmos are therefore alternatives. We cannot create the cosmos—the real meaning is 'beautiful world'—from earthly things but only from chaos by giving form and order to chaos. And anything we do with earthly objects is mere imitation in material form of chaos that has been given order.

That is the case with everything in the sphere of art. In Greece the idea of this relationship between chaos and cosmos was still very much alive under the remaining influence of the culture of the mysteries.

However, when we go about in all these worlds—in the world

where the human being is unconscious when in a state of sleep, and half conscious when in a dream state—if we go anywhere in those worlds, we'll not find the good. The spirits in these worlds have with great wisdom been predetermined from the very beginning of their lives. We find active wisdom prevailing in them and we find beauty in them. But it is pointless to speak of goodness if it is a question of getting to know these spirits when we come to them as earthlings. We can only say goodness when there is a difference between inner and outside world, so that the good can follow the spiritual world or not follow it.

The sleep state is assigned to the truth, the dream state to beauty, and the waking state to goodness, to the good.

Sleep state	*truth**
Dream state	*beauty*
Waking state	*goodness*

This does not go against what I have been saying these days, which is that when we leave the earthly sphere and go out into the cosmos we are also made to let go of earthly concepts and speak of a moral world order. For the moral world order is predetermined in the spiritual sphere, of necessity, just as causality is here on earth. Except that there it is spiritual, predetermination, being well-defined in itself. No contradiction, therefore.

But when it comes to human nature we have to understand that if we want to have the idea of truth we have to turn to the sleep state, if we want to have the idea of beauty we must turn to the dream state, and if we want to have the idea of goodness we must turn to the waking state.

In the waking state, human beings are therefore not determined according to truth, but according to goodness in their physical and etheric organism. So this is where we must really come to the idea of goodness in that case.

---

* In earlier editions, the word 'chaos' had been added to the table. A careful look at the drawing has shown, however, that the word had been written on the board earlier, that is, when Rudolf Steiner used it in the preceding part of his lecture.

Now I would ask you: What are the aims in modern science when people want to explain the human being? Seeking to explain the human being in the waking state, one does not move up from truth to beauty and then goodness. The aim is to explain everything according to an external causal necessity, and this is only in accord with the idea of truth. There we do not arrive at the life and activity in the human being but only at something which at best is only the sleeping human being. So if you read books on anthropology today and do so with an eye that is awake, awake to the soul qualities and powers of the world, the impression you gain is as follows. You say to yourself: 'Well, it is very nice what we are told about the human being in modern science. But what is this human being of which we are told in science really like? He is lying in bed all the time. For he is unable to walk. He cannot move. For movement is absolutely not explained, for instance. So he lies in bed all the time.'

The human being presented in science can only be explained as someone lying in bed. Nothing else is possible. Only the sleeping human being is explained in science. One would have to use mechanical means to set him in motion. This also means that science is a mechanism. Machinery has to be put into this sleeping human being to get this floppy sack moving and out of bed and put him to bed again at night.

Science thus tells us nothing at all about the human being who walks about, is alive and active, is awake. For the principle that sets him in motion lies in the idea of goodness and not the idea of the truth that we initially gain from external objects. This is something to which people do not give much thought. When a present-day physiologist or anatomist gives one a description of the human being one really feels like saying: 'Wake up, wake up; you're asleep, you really are asleep!' Under the influence of this philosophy of life people get used to being in a state of sleep. I have had to say again and again that people are really sleeping through all kinds of things because they are obsessed with science. With popular papers spreading everything far and wide, even people with little education are obsessed with science today. Never before have so many people been obsessed; they are obsessed with science. It is really strange how one has to speak when one has to describe the real situation today. One has to use a very different language than the language that is generally used today.

That is also how it is when someone is introduced a little into the world around him by the materialists. When materialism was at its height, people wrote such books as the one, for instance, which in one particular chapter said: 'Man as such is really nothing. He is the product of the oxygen in the air, he is the product of the low or high temperature in which he finds himself. He is really'—thus the pathetic ending of this materialistic description—'the outcome of every breath of air.'

If one goes into this and imagines someone who really is what the materialistic scientist is saying there, then it is someone who is utterly neurasthenic. The materialists have never described any other kind of human being. They failed to realize that they were actually describing human beings in their sleep, and when they acted in an untypical way and wanted to move on they never described anything but people who were to a high degree neurasthenic and who would have to die the very next day from all that neurasthenia, being quite unable to live. The science of this age has never provided real insight into the living human being.

This is where the great tasks lie which have to guide humanity out of present-day conditions into conditions which are the only ones under which world history can live on. What is needed is that we penetrate into spirituality. The opposite pole must be found to what has been achieved so far. What has really been achieved, especially in the course of the nineteenth century which has been so glorious from the materialistic point of view?

In a wonderful way—we may truly and honestly say so—it has proved possible to determine the outside world according to measure, number and weight as earthly world. Tremendous, magnificent achievements have been made in this respect in the nineteenth and early twentieth centuries. But the sensory perceptions—colours and sounds—are just fluttering around indeterminately.

Physicists no longer speak of colours and sounds; they speak of air waves and ether waves which are neither colour nor sound. Air waves are not sounds. At most they are the medium on which sounds travel. And there is no understanding of sensory qualities. This is something we'll have to come back to again. Essentially people only see things that can be weighed, measured or calculated. The rest escapes them.

When the theory of relativity then also creates the grand disorder of which I spoke yesterday for anything that can be measured, weighed and counted, everything breaks up and falls apart. There are limits, however, boundaries where the theory of relativity fails. Not in its concepts—you cannot escape the theory of relativity if you use earthly concepts; I spoke of this on another occasion—but if you use reality you will always escape from the concepts of relativity. For anything that can be measured, counted and weighed does because of measure, number and weight enter into quite specific relationships in the outside reality perceived through the senses.

A physicist or a number of physicists in Stuttgart once objected to the way in which anthroposophists spoke of the theory of relativity. During a discussion this physicist did the simple experiment to show that it is really quite irrelevant if I have the matchbox here and strike the match against it: it will burn. Or if I keep the match still and move the matchbox against it: it will also burn. It is relative.

Yes, of course, here it will still be relative. And with regard to anything relating to a Newtonian space, or a Euclidean space,[13] all of it will be relative. But as soon as we come to the reality which presents as heaviness, as weight, it is no longer as easy as Einstein imagined it, for then relations are real. One really has to be paradoxical in this case. Relativity can be shown to be valid where one confuses the reality as a whole with mathematics and geometry and mechanics. But this will no longer work when one comes to genuine reality. For surely it is not just relative whether I eat the roast veal or the roast veal eats me! You can do this one way round or the other with a matchbox, but you have to eat the roast veal—you cannot let the roast veal eat you. So there are situations where these concepts of relativity have their limits. The point is that when one says this in the world at large people will say: 'Absolutely lacks all insight into this serious theory.' But the logic of it is the way I said: it is just like that; I cannot change it.

It is a matter, therefore of seeing how if we are taking account of the weight—that is of the quality which really makes it a physical body—we cannot really bring in colours, sounds and so on anywhere in a real way, I'd say. And this tendency means that we have lost something which is extraordinarily important. We have lost the artistic element. This goes away as we grow more and more physical. No one will find even a trace of art in the physics books today. Nothing is left of art; all of it has to go out. It is quite horrible to study a book on physics today if one still has the least sense of beauty. With everything which makes up beauty, using colour and sound, with all of that being outlawed, only given recognition when it is attached to things that have weight, humanity is losing art. Art has been lost today. And the more people go into physics the more inartistic do they grow. Just consider, we have a magnificent science of physics. And there is no need for the opposition to tell us so. As anthroposophists we do say that we have a magnificent science of physics. But physics lives by repudiating the artistic element. In every single aspect it lives by repudiating the artistic element, for in physics one has come to treat the world in a way where the artist does not take the least account of the physicist.

I do not believe, for instance, that musicians consider it worth-while today to study the physical theories on acoustics. They find that boring and not of any concern to them. Nor will a painter be inclined to study the dreadful theory of colours which one finds in physics. If he does at all want to know about colours he will as a rule turn to Goethe's theory of colours. The physicists say that Goethe's theory is wrong, however, but they'll shrug their shoulders and say: 'Ah well, it does not really matter if painters adopt the right or the wrong theory of colour.' The point is that art must perish if today's physical view of the world reigns. So we have to ask ourselves: Why did art exist in earlier times?

If we go back to very early times, to times when human beings still had an original clairvoyance, people were not so much aware of the measure, number and weight of things on earth. They did not really care much for measure, number and weight; they were more inclined to give themselves up to the colours and sounds of things on earth.

Just remember that weight has only been considered since Lavoisier[14] in chemistry—for a little more than a hundred years! Weight was first applied in a philosophy of life at the end of the eighteenth century. Those early human beings simply were not aware that everything has to be determined according to earthly measure, number and weight. They were given up in heart and mind to the tapestry of colours, the waves and movements of sound in the world—not the air waves but the waves and movements of sound. This is what they gave themselves up to. They lived in these things also when living in the physical world.

What potential lay in this way of living in sensory perception free from all weight? It made it possible, for instance, to see a person one was approaching not the way people are seen today but one would look at the person as something which had been brought about by the whole universe. The human being was more a coming together of the cosmos. He would be more of a microcosm than everything that is within his skin on the small bit of ground on which he would be standing. They were more seeing a reflection of the world in a human being. Colours would flow in from all sides to give the human being his colours. The harmony of the world was there, sounding through the human being, giving him his form.

Today it is almost impossible to understand what the teachers in the ancient mysteries told their disciples. For when someone wants to explain the human heart today he takes an embryo and sees how the blood vessels bud and at first there is a tube, with the heart gradually taking shape. That is not how the teachers in the ancient mysteries spoke to their pupils. They would have considered it no more important than what goes on when you knit a sock, for ultimately the process seems much the same. But they put emphasis on something which they considered tremendously important. They would say: 'The human heart is the outcome of the gold which lives

Fig. 4

everywhere in the light, gold which comes streaming in from the universe and actually creates the human heart.' The way they saw it was this: Light moves through the universe and the light bears the gold [Fig. 4]. Gold is everywhere in the light, it is alive and active in the light. And during life on earth the human heart—as you know, it changes every seven years—is not made up of the cucumbers and lettuce and roast veal which people have been eating but, and the ancient teachers knew it, of the gold in the light. The cucumbers and the lettuce merely provide an impulse so that the gold which lives in the light makes up the heart out of the whole universe.

Yes, people put things in a different way and we must become aware of this difference for we have to learn to speak the way they did again, except that it will be at a different level of conscious awareness. In the past, painters painted out of the universe, for things did not have weight then. This has gone; last traces can still be seen with Cimabue, for instance, and above all in the Russian icons. The icon is still painted out of the outer world, out of the macrocosm; it is a detail from the macrocosm. Then, however, a dead end was reached. It was not possible to go any further, because humanity simply no longer had the eye for it. To be inwardly involved in painting the icon and not just do so in the traditional way, one would have needed to know how to treat the gold. The treatment given to the gold in the painting was one of the greatest secrets in the art of painting. To let the human form arise against the background of gold—that was the old way of painting.

There is a vast abyss between Cimabue[15] and Giotto.[16] Giotto was already beginning to do something which Raphael[17] then took to a particular height. Cimabue still had it from tradition, Giotto was halfway turning into a naturalist. He realized that the tradition did no longer come alive in the soul. So one must now take the physical human being, for one no longer had the universe. It was no longer possible to let the painting arise from the gold; one had to base oneself on the flesh.

Finally this went so far that painting widely came to be what it was in the nineteenth century. The icons were weightless, 'shone in' from the world; they had no weight. One cannot paint them any more today, but when they were painted in their original form they would have had no weight at all.

Giotto first began to paint things so that they had weight. As time went on it was so that everything one painted had weight also in the painting, and it would then be coloured from outside; colours then related to the things that were in the paintings so as to be in accord with the physicists' idea that the colour arises there on the surface, due to some particular wave movement. In the end art was also reckoning with the weight. Giotto did, however, begin in an aesthetic, artistic way, and Raphael took it to its greatest height.

We may say, therefore, that the universe was lost to humanity at that point and the weighty human being came to be the only thing one was able to see. The feelings of earlier times were still there, and so the flesh had as little weight as possible, but it did grow heavy. Then the Madonna appeared as the counterpart to the icon—the icon which was weightless, the Madonna who had weight, however beautiful she might be. The beauty survived. But icons can now no longer be painted at all, for human beings have no living experience of them. It is not true when people believe themselves to have living experience of icons today. Which is also why icon culture was touched by a degree of sentimental untruthfulness. That is a dead end in art; it became schematic and traditional.

Raphael's art, which really was based on what Giotto had made of Cimabue, this could only continue to be art for as long as the ancient glory of beauty still rested on it. In a way it was the sunny painters of the Renaissance who were still somewhat sentient of the gold that lived in the light and at least gave their paintings the lustre, letting the gold living in the light shine on them from outside.

That came to an end, however. Naturalism arose. And in art humanity finds itself sitting between two chairs today, on the ground between icon and Madonna, and will have to find a way of discovering pure, actively moving colour and tone, with weight, measurability and weighable numerability the opposite. We must learn to paint out of colour. However tentative and poor our attempts may be, it is our challenge to paint out of colour, to gain living experience of the colour as such, free from all weight. We must be able to proceed in full awareness, full artistic awareness, with these things.

When you look at what we were aiming at in the simple attempts on our programmes[18] you will realize it may only be a beginning, but at least a start has been made in freeing colours from weight, gaining living experience of colour as something which is self-sustaining, and letting the colours speak to us. If this can be achieved, an art will be created in contrast to that inartistic physical view of the world which makes all art evaporate, by taking the free element of colour, of sound and having an art again which is free from gravity.

Yes, we are sitting between the two chairs of icon and Madonna, but we must get up. The science of physics will not help us in this. As I told you, if one applies only physical science to the human being one will always have to remain lying in bed. But now we must get up! And for this we truly need science of the spirit. This has the element of life which takes us from weight, gravity, to colour which is weightless, from being bound up even in musical naturalism to an art of music that is free, and so forth.

We can see everywhere how we need to gather ourselves up, the need for humanity to wake up. We should take up this impulse to come awake, to look out and see what is and is not, and where the challenges are everywhere, to move ahead. This is what I really intended before this summer break occasioned by the visit to England; I had to want to do both at the delegate conference, and now in these days to conclude with the very thoughts which I presented to you. These things do touch a nerve in our time. And it is necessary that we let the other element shine into our movement, which is what I have tried to suggest.

I have told you how the philosopher of the present time has come to admit to himself: 'Where does this intellectualism take us? To build a giant machine at the centre of the earth so that it will make the earth explode out into all the spaces in the universe!' He admitted to himself that that is the situation. The others are not admitting it to themselves.

I have tried, therefore, to show on all kinds of occasions—for instance when I showed you yesterday how concepts that still existed 30 or 40 years ago are today dissolved away by the theory of relativity, simply melting away like snow in the sun—to show that we are indeed challenged everywhere to find our way to anthroposophy. The philosopher Eduard von Hartmann[19] says: 'If the world is the way we have to imagine it to be'—meaning as he has to imagine it in the nineteenth-century sense—'we cannot bear to continue in it and so we must really make it explode out into cosmic space, and it is merely a matter of reaching the point one day when we can do so. We must be longing for the time when we can make the world explode out into the whole wide universe.' Before that, the relativists will see to it that human beings no longer have any concepts. Space, time, motion dissolve, and this can indeed lead to such despair that under certain circumstances one will consider that the greatest satisfaction will lie in thus making our world explode into the whole universe. It is necessary for us to understand clearly the particular impulses that pertain to our age.

Because of this the last lectures had to be given exactly the form which was given to them, letting external culture shine into our ranks. They were also a challenge for you to open your eyes. And I tried to make these lectures such that one could see what it means when we say that the Anthroposophical Society must make every effort to avoid all sectarianism, to rise above sectarianism.

It would be good, my friends, if you were to use the time when I have to be away now for a few weeks to reflect on how one will get out of this sectarianism. Otherwise the situation simply will be that the Anthroposophical Society gets caught up more and more in sectarianism. And there are clear signs not of casting sectarianism aside but of sailing full tilt into a sectarian approach.

We must exercise our minds to see how sectarianism can be avoided. I wanted to refer to this briefly again because it is really most important to refer to it. I wanted to make you aware of how particularly in these last lectures I have tried to speak in such a way that people will everywhere look out into the world, as it were, not cocooning ourselves in a sect but living in the world with open eyes, a practical approach, being part of the world. That is absolutely conformable with entering most deeply into the spiritual sphere. I have therefore told you that today people must even know that it is possible for an Indian, Ramanathan, to look at European civilization and tell the Europeans: 'Ask for teachers about Jesus to come from India, for you really do not understand Jesus Christ at all. We only came to understand the matter when we started to read the New Testament.'

If we want to be sectarian, as there was evidence for this at the delegate conference, we shall not manage the great task which anthroposophy faces at the present time—and it must be managed, for it concerns the whole of humanity.

I hope this has touched your hearts as I now say goodbye for a few weeks. We will announce future events in the usual way. During the next few weeks, there will be lectures and eurythmy performances in various places in England.[20]

So let us now prepare for a summer break in such a way that we let our hearts be very much alive and develop proper sentience of this: How should we feel so that the evolution of humanity may proceed in the right and proper way?

Part Two

MAN AS THE IMAGE OF COSMIC SPIRITS
AND THEIR ACTIVITIES

Lecture 4

It is a real pleasure for me to give this talk here in our London branch[21] after the two conferences in Ilkley and Penmaenmawr[22] which have given me great satisfaction.

When I gave talks here on earlier occasions I did mention that when human beings do their daily work here on earth, day after day and year after year, they are able to do so thanks to their physical bodily nature which was given to them and which connects them physically with their existence on earth. Considering everything which surrounds us here in the physical world during existence on earth, and everything our work contributes to the existing physical world, we must, of course, focus our attention on the time when human beings are awake here on earth. But I also mentioned that what happens to people at the times that they spend in sleep during their life on earth is more important for human existence and, indeed, for anything human beings also have the potential to be in their existence on earth.

When at some time or other in our life on earth we look back on anything we are able to remember, we do really always exclude the times we spent in sleep. We link together everything we have done or experienced during the day, in the waking state, and make it into a coherent whole, as it were.

But this would never exist if the states of sleep did not come in between. To get to know the true nature of the human being we have to pay attention to these sleep states. For people might easily say: 'I do not know anything about what goes on during sleep.' This may seem probable to a superficial view, but it is really untrue when we consider the real situation. We would actually be automatons if we were to look back on a life that was never interrupted by sleep. We would be spiritual but automatons.

The times when we sleep as very young children are even more important than the sleep states that come between our days, for the effects of that infant sleep remain for life. We merely add what mind and spirit gain every night in later life to round them off, as it were. We would be automatons if we were to enter wide awake into the world in our infancy, and in such an automatic state we also would not be in a position to do anything in conscious awareness. Nor would we recognize anything that we did automatically as being our responsibility. When we say we do not remember anything which we have slept through that is in fact not entirely true. As we look back, with the sleep states always dropping out of recollection, we actually, in looking back on a nothing, see the events we experienced in our waking hours in one way or another at the points in time when we were asleep. In fact, however, we see nothing at those points in time. If you have a white wall and there is a place on it where there is no colour but a black circle, you are also seeing a nothing. You see the dark bit, or if it is not a black circle but a hole with no light behind it, if you like, you will see a hole. You see the darkness. That is how you see the darkness in your life as you look back. The times where you were asleep appear to be life's darknesses. And you call these dark-nesses 'I'. You would not be aware of your I if you did not see these darknesses. You do not owe the ability to say 'I' to yourself to the fact that you have always been working from morning to night; you owe it to the fact that you did sleep. For the I, as we refer to it in earthly existence, is first of all the darkness in life, the emptiness, the non-existence. If we look at our life in the right way we do not have to say that we owe our self-awareness to the day. We owe it to the night. And so it is really only the night which makes us into real human beings, where otherwise we'd just be automatons.

It truly is the case that going back to earlier times in human evolution on earth we see that human beings were not automatons because there were already some differences between waking and sleeping. They were, however, more or less aware of their sleep states even in their ordinary daytime state of mind and because of this their actions, the whole of their life on earth was much more automatic than the life which people live on earth in the present time.

We are therefore able to say that our real, true inner I is something we actually do not really bring with us into this physical earth world. We always leave it in the spiritual world. It was in the spiritual world before we came down into earthly existence. It is back in the spiritual world between our going to sleep and waking up. It always stays in the spiritual world. When we have our present-time conscious awareness as human beings during the day and call ourselves 'I', this word 'I' is a reference to something which does not exist in this physical world, though there is an image of it in this physical world.

We do not have the right view of ourselves when we say: 'I am this robust person on earth, standing here as I truly am.' We only have the right view of ourselves if we say: 'What exists here on earth is an image, truly an image of our true nature.' To be absolutely correct we should not regard this entity here on earth as the genuine human being but only as the image of the genuine human being.

This image character can be more clearly understood if we consider the following. Imagine we are asleep. The I has gone away from the physical body and the ether body, the astral body has gone away from the physical body and ether body. But the I is active in the blood and in the movements of a human being. These activities cease when the I is away during sleep. But the element that is in the blood does continue to be active; the I is not there at all. We only have to look at this physical body and we have to say to ourselves: 'What is the situation there when we are asleep?' The blood must then, too, have something active in it, just as during the day the I is alive in it. The same applies to the astral body which always lives in the whole breathing process. During the night it leaves the breathing process, but the breathing process continues! There must be something in there as well that acts as the astral body does in daytime life. In sleep life, our astral body leaves the organs in us which are our respiratory organs, for instance. Our I leaves the powers that make the blood pulsate. Now what do they do during the night? Well, the situation is that when the individual has been lying in bed, with his I departing from the blood-pulsating powers, spirits from the next higher hierarchy enter into the blood-pulsating powers. Angeloi, Archangeloi and Archai then live in the self-same organs in which the I lives during the waking hours of the day. And the spirits of the next higher hierarchy are during the night active in the respiratory organs from which we departed because our astral body has left us: Exusiai, Dynamis, Kyriotetes.

So the situation is that when our I and astral body depart from our daytime bodily nature as we go to sleep at night, angels, archangels and higher spirits enter into us and give life to our organs while we sleep, until we wake up again. When it comes to the ether body, we are not even able to do what needs to be done in there during our waking hours. The spirits of the highest hierarchy, Seraphim, Cherubim and Thrones, must be present in it even in our waking hours; they are altogether always present in it.

And then the physical body! If we had to manage all the magnificent, tremendous processes in our physical body ourselves we would not only do this badly but we would not at all know how to set about it; we'd be quite helpless. The things said about the physical body in external anatomy would not be able to set a single atom of it in motion. This calls for very different powers.

These powers are none other than those which have from time immemorial been known as the powers of the highest trinity, Father, Son and Spirit, the actual Trinity which dwells in our physical body.

So we are able to say that throughout our life on earth the physical body is not ours; it would not go through its development under our direction. As has been said in ancient times, it is the temple of the godhead, the godhead which is a trinity. Our ether body is the dwelling place of the hierarchy of Seraphim, Cherubim and Thrones; those of our organs which are assigned to the ether body must be taken care of also by Seraphim, Cherubim and Thrones. The physical and ether organs we have, from which the astral body departs during the night, must be taken care of by the second hierarchy—Kyriotetes, Dynamis and Exusiai. And those of our organs from which the I departs must during the night be cared for by the third hierarchy, by Angeloi, Archangeloi and Archai.

So there is constant activity in the human being which is not only his own effort. He is really only a subtenant in his organism during waking hours. This organism of his is at the same time the temple and dwelling place of the spirits belonging to the higher hierarchies.

Giving this our consideration we can say: 'We are really only taking the right view of the outer human form when we say to ourselves that it is an image reflecting the activities of all the hierarchies. They are in there. And when I look at this head in its human form with all its details, the rest of the body in its human form, I do not see it in the right way if I say it is this or that entity but only if I say it is an image of an invisible supersensible activity of all the hierarchies.' We have to look at these things in this way before we are saying the right things, in detail, of something which is otherwise always only presented in a highly abstract way.

People say that this physical world is not real, it is Maya, and the reality is behind it. But you cannot do much with that. It is merely a general truth, just like saying that there are flowers growing in the meadow. We can only do something when we know what kind of flowers are growing in the meadow. In the same way we can only do something with knowledge of the higher world if we are able to show in detail how the higher world is active in something which outwardly appears as an image, as Maya, an echo, a revelation in the physical world which is perceived through the senses.

Seen as a whole, therefore, in his life during the day and also during the night on earth man relates not only to his physical environs, which he perceives through the senses when on earth, but also to the world of higher spirituality. A certain, we might say lower spirituality is active throughout the realms of nature here on earth— the mineral, vegetable and animal worlds. The actions of the higher spirituality, which influences man, come from the world of stars. Because of his physical existence the human being as a whole does here on earth relate to the plants and animals, to water and air. And as a whole the human being also relates to the world of the stars which on their part are also only image, revelation of something that exists in reality. And it is in reality that those spirits of the higher hierarchies exist. Looking up to the stars we are essentially looking up to the spirits of the higher hierarchies which merely let something like a symbolic light of their existence shine out to us, so that in physical existence, too, we get a hint of the spiritual principle that essentially fills the whole of the universe.

Here on earth we have a certain longing to really know the mountain, the river, the animal, the plant. And we should really also have a longing to gain genuine insight into the world of stars as it truly is. In Penmaenmawr I gave some indications concerning the spiritual nature of the moon just as it shines down on us from cosmic space at this particular stage of earth evolution.

Looking at the moon, we actually never see the moon itself but at most only a faint hint where the illuminated sickle continues, just as we do always only see reflected sunlight and never the moon itself. Forces from the universe are reflected back to reach us on earth and not something which lives in the moon itself. It is just part, the smallest part, of what belongs to the moon that it reflects the sunlight down onto the earth. In reality it acts like a mirror, reflecting back to us all the physical and spiritual impulses that influence it from the universe. And just as we do not see what is at the back of the mirror, so we never see the inner part of the moon, though there is a genuine spiritual population inside the moon, with sublime guiding spirits. Those guiding spirits and the rest of the moon's population have once been here on earth. They withdrew from the earth to the moon at a time which was more than 15,000 years ago. Before that, the moon also had a different physical appearance. It did not simply send down the sun's light to the earth, but blended its own essential nature into this sunlight. Well, this need not concern us so much. But we should be interested in the fact that today the moon is like a fastness in the universe. And in this fastness lives a population which went through human destinies more than 15,000 years ago and has withdrawn to this moon with the spirits that guide humanity.

There was a time in the past when advanced spirits existed on earth who did not assume a physical human body as we do now but lived more in an etheric body. Yet they were nevertheless the great teachers and educators of humanity at that time.

These great teachers and educators of humanity who at one time brought original wisdom to human beings on earth, sublime original elements of wisdom worthy of our admiration, with the Vedas and Vedanta only echoes of them, live inside the moon today and let the things that live outside of the moon in the universe shine down onto the earth.

Something of those moon powers has remained behind on earth; but those are only the physical powers of procreation for human beings and animals. Only the outermost physical aspect remained behind when in ancient Atlantean times the great teachers of humanity followed the moon, which had even before that withdrawn from the earth.

Looking up to the moon we therefore see the reality of it only if we understand that sublime spirits who were once connected with the earth are today making it their task to reflect back on to the earth not what they bear within themselves but such physical forces and spiritual powers as are mediated in the universe. Anyone seeking to gain initiation wisdom today must above all also seek to include in this initiation wisdom the things that the moon spirits are able to tell them, being endowed with higher powers.

Well, that is one figure, as it were, out there in the universe, a colony, a settlement. Others are equally important, especially those which are part of our planetary system. I'd say that at the other pole, the other extreme with regard to this importance for us human beings on earth, is the population on Saturn.

The Saturn population was not connected with the earth in the same way as the moon population. There was a connection, and you can read about this in my *Occult Science, an Outline*. But the Saturn spirits are not connected with the earthly sphere in the same way as the moon spirits, for they do not reflect anything which exists in cosmic space. We get scarcely even physical sunlight reflected by Saturn. The planet travels slowly around the sun like a solitary, not very luminous hermit. Yet everything external astronomy can tell us about Saturn is just the very least of it. The significance which Saturn has for humanity on earth shows itself every night, but only as an image, and particularly also in the life between death and rebirth, when human beings pass through the spiritual and hence the star world. I have spoken of this before in a lecture I gave to this branch.[23]

Human beings do not meet the actual Saturn at the present stage of human evolution, but do nevertheless meet with the Saturn spirits in a roundabout way. I will not go into this today. But the point is that the spirits who dwell inside Saturn have reached a very high level of perfection, extreme sublimity. These spirits have a direct inner relationship to Seraphim, Cherubim and Thrones. Seraphim, Cherubim and Thrones are really the spirits of the hierarchy right next to their own.

These spirits, this population of Saturn, really do not let anything shine down from Saturn to earth and do not give human beings anything from the outer physical world. On the other hand the Saturn spirits retain cosmic memory, cosmic remembrance. Everything which the planetary system has gone through physically and spiritually, anything which spirits in our planetary system have lived through, is faithfully retained as memory by the Saturn spirits. Those spirits are always looking back on the whole life of the planetary system in remembrance. We look back on the whole of our narrow life on earth in memory; Saturn spirits have—together in their activities—cosmic remembrance of everything which the whole has gone through and also every individual entity in the planetary system. And all the powers which live in this remembrance are alive for human beings because they connect with these Saturn spirits between death and rebirth, and in image form actually also every night. It is thanks to this that the powers which come from those Saturn spirits, which actually represent the most profound inner life of the planetary system, are active in human beings. Memory is the deepest innermost part of us when on earth, and in Saturn there really lives the deepest innermost cosmic I of the whole planetary system.

It is because these activities exist in human beings that events come in life, most of the significance of which does not come to awareness, which nevertheless play the greatest imaginable role in the life of a person. Most of what we are aware of in life is actually the least that there is in life.

When there is some major event at some point in life—you have for instance met someone with whom you will then be together for the rest of your life, or some other truly significant event—and you look back from this point you will find that it strikes you that it is like a plan which has been guiding you towards this event for a long time. It is sometimes possible with something which comes up in your thirtieth to fiftieth year to go back through your life and you'll find: 'Yes, it was actually when I was ten or twelve years old that I started on the road to this event; everything that came later went in such a way that I finally ended up with this event.

People who have grown old and then look back on their life find, if they are thoughtful, their way about in life to such effect that they are able to say: 'There we have such a subconscious connection. Unconscious powers compel us towards the one event or another.'

These are the Saturn powers, powers implanted in us because we relate in the way I have indicated to the population which is inside Saturn.

Now if on the one hand only the physical powers of procreation exist on earth as having remained behind from the moon, then on the other hand the most sublime powers, relating to cosmic morality, are on earth thanks to Saturn. Saturn is the greatest equalizer for all events on earth. Whereas the moon powers, as they are now on earth, have to do only with heredity from the father, mother, and so on, the Saturn powers relate to what lives in karma in our human life, passing from incarnation to incarnation. And the other planets are in between, mediating the physical and the most sublime moral principle.

Between the moon and Saturn we then have Jupiter, Mars and so on. They have their own way of conveying the things which the moon and Saturn, the outermost extremes, bring into human life—the moon because its spirits have withdrawn, leaving only the physical aspect of activities on earth, the physical power of procreation, and Saturn as the most sublime moral justice in the universe. The two act together, and the other planets between the two of them interweave the one element and the other. Karma mediated by Saturn, physical heredity mediated by the moon—they alone show how in progressing from one life on earth to another human beings are connected with the earth itself and with all that exists in the universe outside the earth.

It is understandable that modern physical science, being concerned only with earthly existence, really can say only very little about the human being. There is much about the powers of heredity but no realization that they are powers left behind by the moon. Physicists do not know how to relate them to their activities outside the earthly sphere, nor that karma also influences human life as the destiny that continues from one life on earth to the next, and that the spirits which bear within them the great remembrance of the whole planetary system and its events are sending their pulses through it, just as the blood pulses through us as physical human beings. Let us look into ourselves. We are human beings only because we have memory. Looking at the planetary system with all that goes on in it both physically and spiritually, we must say, if we want to attain to initiation wisdom: The whole of this planetary system would really have no inwardness if the population of Saturn did not all the time preserve the memory, the past, of this planetary system, continually also letting the powers which grow from such preservation of the past enter into humanity, so that all these human beings live from one life on earth to another in a living spiritual and moral causal connection.

In life on earth human beings are in their relationship to others kept within narrow limits for the things they do consciously. If they consider, however, what they go through between death and rebirth, their relationship to others is within a wider compass, those others then also being out of body, not within a physical body. Yes, between death and rebirth human beings are at one time closer to the moon influences, we may say, at another time closer to the influences of Saturn, Mars and so on, but one kind of power always influences the other powers through cosmic spaces. Here on earth we can only do things as one human being to another through narrowly confined earth spaces. Between death and rebirth our actions extend from planet to planet. The universe truly is the arena then for human activities and also the relationships between human beings. One human soul might be within the Venus sphere, the other within the Jupiter sphere between death and rebirth, but their interactions are of greater inwardness than is possible on earth, where the degree is limited. Between death and rebirth vast cosmic distances are called into the arena of interactions between human souls. And the spirits of the higher hierarchies also act through such vast spaces. Because of this we can speak not only of the actions of individual kinds of spirits—let us say the Venus or the Mars population—but also of a continuous to and fro of powers or forces between the Mars population and the Venus population in the universe.

Everything that thus happens in the universe between the Mars population and the Venus population, all the interactions, everything that lives in the cosmos, in the spiritual cosmos as the mutually fructifying acts of Mars and Venus also relates to the human being. Saturn memory relates to human karma; the physical moon powers that were left behind relate to the physical powers of procreation, and the hidden things that happen all the time between Mars and Venus relate to human speech and language here on earth. Purely physical powers would not enable us to speak. The power of speech also shines out from the essential nature of the human being, which has its existence from life on earth to life on earth, which has its life between death and rebirth. During the time when we live as spirits between death and rebirth we also enter into the mode of action which is so fructifying between Mars and Venus, between the Mars population and the Venus population. These powers which shine out in the one direction and the other, this way of working together, has its influence on us in our life between death and rebirth. It then comes to fruition in the physical image. This is the element which enters into our organs of speech and song, coming from the most inward development as human beings.

We would not be able to speak, using our organs of speech and song, if they were not physically stimulated by the powers that we take in with the depths of our being between death and rebirth from something which goes to and fro between Mars and Venus in the cosmos.

In the things we do every day we are thus under the influence of the powers of the stars, seeing only their signs as we look up to them in wonder and awe. One has to know that the stars shining down on us from space are really only the characters, signs, representing the most universal spiritual activity that lives in us and of which we are the image. Only if we do so can we look up to the stars in the right way.

An earlier humanity could use an atavistic clairvoyance to gain such vision, but that way of looking has gradually faded away. Human beings could not have grown free if they had stayed with the old way of seeing. This turned dark and instead the Mystery on Golgotha entered into life on earth. A sublime spirit from the sun population could give human beings not immediate awareness of what is going on in the world of the stars, but the powers needed for gradually gaining this kind of conscious awareness.

The situation therefore was that to begin with, at the time when the Mystery on Golgotha took place, an ancient hereditary Gnostic wisdom existed which allowed people to grasp the Mystery on Golgotha. This vanished in the fourth century BC. The power which had come to earth through the Christ has remained. And human beings can bring this power to life in themselves by taking up what the more recent spiritual science can say and opening their eyes again to the spiritual worlds.

This eye for the spiritual worlds will mean many things for the human race of more recent times. It is, after all, a strange thing that the people who still have something of the old instinctive wisdom— which in the best sense of the word is no longer right for our time and must be superseded by a conscious wisdom—that the people over yonder in the Orient who have retained something of the wisdom in all kinds of different regions in Asia and are the educated people, the scholars there, are really looking down on Europe and America in a disparaging way. They are convinced that even in its present state of decline their ancient Asian wisdom, or really rather the bits and pieces of it, are still better than all the things that make Western civilization so arrogant. And it is certainly interesting that it was possible for such a book to appear like that of an Indian in Ceylon entitled *The Culture of the Soul among Western Nationals.*[24] This Sinhalese Indian is telling the Europeans nothing less but: 'Since the Middle Ages your knowledge of the Christ has become extinct. You do not have any real knowledge of the Christ today, for only someone who is able to look into the spiritual world can have genuine knowledge of the Christ. So you will have to ask teachers to come from India or Asia who will teach you Christianity.' You can read in that book how a Sinhalese Indian is telling the Europeans: 'Ask for teachers to come from Asia; they will be able to tell you what the Christ really is. Your teachers in Europe do not know anything about it any more. From the end of the Middle Ages you have lost your knowledge of the Christ.'

And this is what matters, that the Europeans and Americans do indeed find the courage again to look to those spiritual worlds where knowledge of the Christ, Christ wisdom, can be gained again, for the Christ is the spirit who came down from spiritual worlds into existence on earth. This can only be understood in its true depth by grasping it in the spirit.

It will be necessary for human beings to learn to see themselves truly as an image of higher spirits and spiritual influences here on earth. They can best do this by really taking in the kind of views like those I put before you at the beginning of today's talk, where human beings essentially look at the emptiness in their temporal life and grow aware that the I does not actually come down from the spiritual world, and that the human being is mere image in the physical world, with the I not present in the physical world. They see a hole, as it were, in time, and this hole really seems dark to them. It is to this that they say 'I'.

Human beings should therefore be aware particularly of the most significant fact that when remembering they must look back on their life and say to themselves: 'Yes, going back in memory I see the events of the day, but darkness always appears in it like a hole. This darkness is what I call "I" in my ordinary state of mind. But I must become aware of something else.'

I have summed up this something else in a few words that may be taken to heart by everyone today as a kind of meditation to find the I by more and more often bringing the words to life in us which I would wish to put in this way:

> I look into utter darkness.
> A light shines out,
> Light that is alive.
> Who is this light in the darkness?
> It is my true and real I.
> This does not enter into life on earth.
> I am just an image of it.
> But I shall find it again
> When
> With good will for the spirit
> I shall have gone through the gate of death.

We can enter into such a meditation again and again to face the darkness and understand clearly that on earth we are really only the image of the part of our true nature which never comes down into earthly existence, but that with good will for the spirit a light can arise in the darkness and we may admit to ourselves, 'We ourselves are this light in our reality.'

Part Three

REPORT ON MY VISIT TO ENGLAND [AND WALES] AND THE WORK DONE THERE

Report on my Visit to England [and Wales] and the Work Done There

Dornach, 9 September 1923[25]

My friends, tonight I want to tell you something about the journey. Tomorrow I plan to give one more lecture—the following week I'll have to be in Stuttgart—in which I'll go into some things which as subject matter relate more to the description of the visit which I am giving today.

The visit started in Ilkley, in the north of England, where a course on education was to be given, a course about the Waldorf School method and teaching, with reference to present-day civilization.[26] Ilkley is in the north of England, a place with about 8,000 inhabitants. It is currently the fashion in England to conduct summer schools in such places during the summer months, and this course initially also took the form of such a summer school.

It was to be accompanied by the art of eurythmy we have developed in the anthroposophical movement, and also by contributions of six of our Waldorf School teachers, always on the subject matter of the individual lectures.

Ilkley is considered to be a kind of summer resort. It is, however, very close to the cities which put one right into the industrial and commercial culture of today. Leeds is very close, and other places such as Bradford and Manchester are not far away. These cities absolutely reflect the life which has evolved under present-day conditions. One truly is sentient there of how much our present age needs the spirit to come in. This coming in of the spirit should not be limited, however, to giving something to people for their immediate individual and personal inner needs. It is no doubt perfectly justifiable to see the anthroposophical movement in that particular light, but I am now speaking of impressions which today's outside world is really forcing upon us.

You see, my friends, the situation is that one would feel it to be extraordinarily paradoxical in the cultural world if someone were to recommend adding indigestible mineral products—some kinds of minerals, stones and so on—to human foods, considering it possible to add sand or the like to human food. The ideas which people have of the human organism make us consider this to be impossible. Yet someone able to look more deeply into the way the world is made and the connections which exist in it—it is fair for once to say so out of genuine anthroposophical feeling and sentience—will in a particular sense be sentient of houses and factories put together in a style which may be said to do nothing to meet the aesthetic needs of people. That is the case in Leeds, for instance, where unbelievably black houses are lined up in an abstract way and everything really looks as if it were a straight condensation of the blackest coal dust which has collected together and has come to create houses where people then come to live. Looking at this in conjunction with evolving culture and civilization for the whole of humanity and in the same frame of mind as considering what I have just been saying about sand in the stomach, one really feels one has to say: It is equally impossible for human civilization that such a thing permanently becomes part of the whole course of human evolution and that civilization could makes any kind of inner progress in that case.

It truly is not a question of one ever being a reactionary in basing oneself on anthroposophy. We certainly must not speak of these things in a negative sense. They simply have arisen from the life of the whole of earth evolution. Yet within human evolution they are only possible if a genuine spiritual life enters into them, fills them, and truly enters particularly into these things and gradually becomes able to lift them out into a form of aesthetics, so that people will not be completely removed from an inner humanity because such things have become part of developing civilization.

I'd like to say that it is exactly such an experience which makes one aware of the most absolute need for spiritual impulses to enter into our present civilization. These things cannot be taken to be mere general ideas which one has; no, they must truly be seen in connection with what there is in the world. One has to have a heart, however, for whatever there is in the world.

Ilkley itself is a place the environs of which have the atmosphere on the one hand of these industrial cities being so close. On the other hand there is something everywhere, though only in traces, which in the remnants of dolmens or cromlechs scattered about, of ancient Druid altars,[27] does remind one of ancient spirituality, though nothing remains that follows from it directly. It is touching, I'd say, if on the one hand one is under the impression I have just been describing and on the other hand walks up a hill in this region where the atmosphere of those impressions can certainly still be felt and where in the extraordinarily characteristic sites, wherever they may be, one finds the remnants of the old sacrificial altars with the ancient signs on them. There is something extraordinarily touching about them. One such stone may be found on a hill near Ilkley, and on this stone essentially—it is actually a bit more complicated—but essentially is the sign referred to as a swastika. This was carved into stones positioned in particular sites in the past and refers to something quite specific. It indicates that these were sites where the Druid priest would be full of the thoughts which until, let us say, two or three thousand years ago created the culture in these regions. For

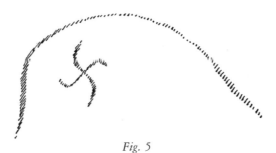

Fig. 5

when you come to such a site and stand before such a rock with the signs engraved in them, you still find from the whole situation today that you are in the place where the Druid priest once stood. The engraved sign would have made him sentient that he brought the state of mind that was in keeping with his position to expression in this sign.

What do we read in this sign when we stand before such a stone? We read the words that lived in the heart of the Druid priest: 'Lo and behold, the eye as a physical sense sees the mountains, sees the people's dwelling places; the eye of the spirit, with the lotus flower, the swastika the sign for it, looks into human hearts, into the inner soul. And with this ability to see I want to be close to the people of this congregation who are entrusted to my care.' Standing before such a stone one reads this, as it were, just as otherwise one reads the written text in a book.

So that was more or less the atmosphere around the Ilkley conference. The programme was that I would always give lectures in the mornings where on this occasion I sought to develop Waldorf Education and teaching out of the whole historical evolution of educational practice. On this occasion I started from the way in which in Greek civilization education grew out of the whole way of life in Greece. We may conclude from this that we should not invent special methods and practices for school, but that school is meant to convey what exists in the given culture.

It certainly is not right, for instance, to invent special practices by the Froebel method[28] in nursery schools—I certainly do not intend to be critical about Froebel—to do various things with the children. Those practices do not relate to cultural life in general and have not evolved from it. No, the right thing is for the practitioner in education to be wholly within cultural life in general, having a heart and a mind for it, and then bringing the life as it is lived, and into which the pupils are meant to grow later on, directly into one's methods of education.

My aim therefore was to show how education and teaching methods may grow naturally from our life, which now, however, is filled with spirit. This made it possible to look at the Waldorf School method from yet another point of view. What I have said just now was merely a starting point; what mattered was to elucidate Waldorf School education, with which you are, of course, familiar.

There followed a eurythmy performance in Ilkley Theatre by the children from Kings Langley School[29] and eurythmy performances by the artists who had come with us. It would probably have been better to have the latter first. Such an arrangement would have made it immediately obvious that the eurythmy done in schools grows out of the art of eurythmy which is part of cultural life. Well, these things will settle down in future, when even the external arrangements will demonstrate what is really intended.

The third element, as it were, comprised the efforts of the Waldorf teachers who had come with us. And here I really have to say that they met with the greatest imaginable interest. I have to say that Dr von Baravalle's[30] effort, for instance, the way in which he did it, was extraordinarily touching when the development of the Waldorf School is dear to one's heart. One saw Dr von Baravalle present his views on geometry as appropriate for children in such a simple way, using the method which you would surely know from his book on methods in physics and mathematics. The evolution—truly artistic—of the transformation and metamorphosis suddenly and with inner drama led to the Pythagorean theorem, and one then saw how the audience was taken along step by step, not really sure as to where all this was leading, with a number of areas moved around again and again until finally the Pythagorean theorem was beautifully illustrated on the blackboard. The audience, made up of teachers, was inwardly amazed, with thoughts and feelings developing with such inner drama and, I would say, such straightforward, evident enthusiasm for a teaching method that it was truly moving—as was everything our teachers presented—and it was met with the most extraordinary interest imaginable. We had brought along students' work—modelling, toy making, painting and so on—and there was enormous interest in hearing how the children work on such things and how it finds its place in the whole school curriculum.

Miss Laemmert's[31] demonstration of the way in which music is taught was followed with the greatest possible attention, as were the words of Dr Schwebsch.[32] The impressive, charming style of Dr von Heydebrand,[33] then the forceful style of our Dr Karl Schubert[34]—all these things really showed that it is possible to present the Waldorf School system most impressively to teachers. Miss Roehrle[35] then gave a eurythmy lesson to a number of people, which rounded things off nicely, with the whole put together really well from the educational point of view. I am permitted to say so, for I had no part at all in creating the programme. It was all brought together so well by our English friends that we really had a very good general presentation of the educational way of presenting subjects.

A committee was then established during the conference with the aim of establishing an independent school on the Waldorf School pattern in England. The prospects of having this as a day school are really very good. Kings Langley School had already declared themselves ready to adopt the Waldorf School method after my Oxford lectures[36] the year before. As I said, the children from Kings Langley had shown in the Ilkley Theatre what they had learned in eurythmy. The interest and attentiveness shown, with the eurythmy performances also warmly received, are something which can truly make one feel great satisfaction. This was in the first half of August, until 18 August. We then moved on to Penmaenmawr.[37]

Penmaenmawr is a place in the north of Wales, on the west coast of England, with the island of Anglesey to the west. No better place could really have been chosen for this anthroposophical undertaking. Penmaenmawr is full of an astral atmosphere that comes to immediate experience. Into it have entered Druid elements, traces of which may still be found everywhere. It lies on the coast, where Anglesey is. A bridge goes across to the island, and this is a piece of real engineering genius. On the one side of the place hills and mountains arise everywhere, and scattered through those mountains everywhere are these remnants of ancient 'sacrificial altars', cromlechs and so on; traces of the ancient Druid worship may be found everywhere.

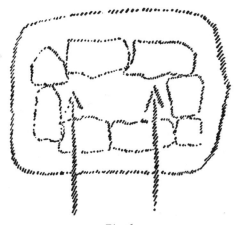

Fig. 6

The scattered individual places appear to be set up in the simplest possible way. Looking from the side, they are stones arranged in a square or rectangle, with one stone on top. Looking from above, these stones would be arranged like this [Fig. 6] and there would be one stone on top which makes the whole into a small chamber.

Such things have no doubt also been burial places. But I would say that in earlier times the function of burial places was always connected with the function of a much more extensive rite. Let me tell you without reserve what such a ritual site can teach us.

You see, the stones enclose a kind of small chamber, with a covering stone above. The chamber is in a particular way in darkness. When the sun's rays reach it, the outer physical light stays behind. But sunlight is always full of flowing spirituality, and this enters into the dark chamber. As an initiate the Druid priest was able to see through the Druid stones and see the stream that went down—not the physical sunlight, for that was blocked out, but the spirit and soul which lives in the physical light of the sun. This would inspire him with something which then entered into his wisdom concerning the spiritual cosmos, the universe. So these were sites not only for burial but also for the gaining of insight.

There is more, however. When the thing I have just described happened at particular times of day we may say: At other times of day something else was the case, for streams would also come back from the earth [arrows pointing upwards] and these could be observed when the sun did not shine on them. In them lives the moral qualities of the priest's congregation. At certain times the priest would therefore be able to see the moral qualities of his parishioners in the area. The spiritual element streaming down and also the spiritual element streaming up showed him what he needed to be truly spiritual in his sphere of activity.

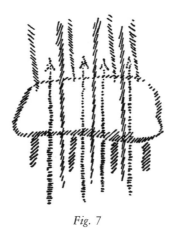

Fig. 7

These things do not, of course, appear in present-day scientific information on those sites. One can, however, see it directly for the power of the impulses—impulses governing the work of Druid priests at the time which was indeed their good time—the impulses were so strong that these things are absolutely still alive in the astral atmosphere in that place.

I was also able to visit a different ancient site with Dr Wachs-muth.[38] From Penmaenmawr you walk up a mountain for about 1½ hours. On top there is a kind of depression [Fig. 8]. From that depression one has a marvellous open view of surrounding mountains and also the boundaries of the depression up there. A site which may be said to be the actual sun ritual site of the ancient Druids was found in that depression. The way it appears is that

Fig. 8

the corresponding stones were set up with their cover leaves;* one sees traces everywhere.

Think of it like this. These ancient sites had no internal space. Up here you find two such Druid circles. When the sun moves through the heavens during the day, the shadows of these stones are at all kinds of different angles. It is possible, we say, to distinguish the Ram shadow when the sun passes through the Ram constellation, and then the Bull shadow, the Twins shadow and so on. Even today, you gain a fair impression in deciphering these things of how the Druid priest was able to read the secrets of the universe in the different sun shadows, different in quality, as they appeared in this Druid circle, in quality which continues to live in the shadow cast by the sun when the physical sunlight is held back. A cosmic clock telling of the secrets of the world did indeed exist in the circle. They were definitely signs that arose in the shadows that were cast, shadows that spoke of the secrets of the world, of the cosmos.

The second circle was like a kind of control, to check on the results of the first circle. If one could have gone up in a plane and far enough

---

* According to the records, Rudolf Steiner said 'with their *Deckblaetter*'. This is a puzzle. The stones are standing stones, with no lintels. If it had been lintels, he might have said *Deckplatten*, but definitely not *Deckblaetter*. I have done extensive researches but found no solution to the problem. The word is made up of two elements: *Deck-*, which means 'cover', 'covering', and *-blaetter*, which means leaves. One possibility would be flaky bits caused by weathering. Both the original shorthand record and the transcript held at the Rudolf Steiner Archive in Dornach consistently state 'Deckblaetter'. Anna R. Meuss.

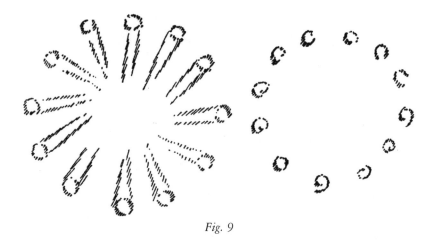

Fig. 9

away that the distance between them might have disappeared, the two Druid circles would actually have given the ground plan for our Goetheanum.

The location is close to Anglesey, an island where many things happened that survive in the tales about King Arthur. His centre was a bit more to the south, but many things also took place here which were part of King Arthur's activities. All this adds something to the astral atmosphere of Penmaenmawr and distinctly makes it into a special place, something of which we may say that speaking of spiritual things we need to do so in images. The situation with thinking in images is that the images created as one speaks of things very soon vanish in the astral atmosphere within our present-day civilization. Seeking to speak of spiritual things one is all the time battling against the disappearance of the images. One has to present these images but they soon fade and one is over and again facing the need to produce the images so that one has them before one. The astral atmosphere which arises from these things in that place is such that whilst it is a bit more difficult to produce the images in Penmaenmawr the difficulties do on the other hand, greatly ease spiritual life, the images once created simply looking as if they were written into the astral atmosphere. When you are there you feel that if you are in some way or other thinking in images that reflect the spiritual world they remain in the astral atmosphere there. This very circumstance reminds one in such a lively way of how those Druid priests selected the special sites where they could effectively, I'd say, engrave as it were in the astral atmosphere the things which it behove them to configure in images derived from the secrets of the cosmos. One does indeed feel it to be like an actual step taken, stepping across a threshold as one is coming across from Ilkley— which is so close to industrialism and only gives a faint indication of ancient Druid times—and now enters into something that is simply spiritual in the immediate present. It is all spiritual.

We can certainly say: Wales is a special place on earth. Today Wales is the preserver of a tremendously powerful spiritual life, consisting, it is true, of memories but real memories which are right there. The possibility of speaking purely about anthroposophy in this place—not in following its offshoots but pre-eminently—is something I consider to be one of the most significant periods in the development of our anthroposophical life.

We are indebted to Mr Dunlop[39] for making these arrangements and now also bringing something of this nature into the evolving anthroposophical life. Full of insight, he has been working with energy. He submitted the plan for it when I was in England last year, stuck to this plan and now had also brought it to realization. From the beginning, the plan had been to present purely anthroposophical subject matter in conjunction with eurythmy in that place in August.

Mr Dunlop also had a third impulse but it was not possible to achieve it, and we may certainly say that such things as did become possible only did so because of the genuine spiritual insight in choosing that particular place. I think it is of some importance to realize that there are such special places on earth, where memory is still very much alive of the sun rites once performed in the north and west of Europe to prepare for the coming of Christianity.

The lectures were given in the mornings; part of the afternoon gave conference members the opportunity to experience on the spot the astral atmosphere and its connection with the memories attached to the ruins of sacrificial sites, dolmen, and so on. In the evenings we had discussions on anthroposophical subjects or eurythmy performances. We had five of those in Penmaenmawr, received with truly great inwardness and also the greatest interest. Some of the audience were anthroposophists, others not. As one would expect in an area close by the sea, the weather changed from hour to hour, semi-cloudbursts alternating with bright sunshine and so forth. There even—the premises were something rather like our woodwork shop here in Dornach—was an evening when people really had to walk through a kind of cloudburst to get to the eurythmy performance; when the performance started they still had their umbrellas up in the hall, but this did not dampen their enthusiasm. It really was something, and I did also say so in Penmaenmawr, which we call a highly significant chapter in the history of our anthroposophical movement.

One event was devoted to a discussion of educational issues also in Penmaenmawr. I would also like to take this occasion to mention the following, which you have already been able to read about in the brief report I gave in *Das Goetheanum*. When I arrived in Ilkley, a book entitled *Education Through Imagination*[40] was waiting for me and captivated me quite extraordinarily even when I first glanced through it. One of our friends in particular called it one of the most important books in England. The author is Miss McMillan. She was actually taking the chair for the first evening and those that followed in Ilkley. Miss McMillan gave the opening address. It was uplifting to see this woman's marvellous enthusiasm and honest inner fire for the practice of education. At the same time we felt an extraordinarily great satisfaction that this particular woman is fully acknowledging the things that can be achieved with Waldorf School methods, an approach to teaching practice based on truly serious intent.

Having read the book fully in the days that followed I summed up my impressions in the article which appeared in the last issue of *Das Goetheanum*.[41] On the last Monday my wife and I were then able to visit the centre of this excellent lady's activities in Deptford, near London, near Greenwich. That is where Miss McMillan has her day-centre.[42] She takes the children from the lowest, poorest classes; she intends to take older children as well. Today there are 300 children; she started many years ago with six, and today there are 300. The children come first when two years old, from areas where they are really dirty, neglected, sick, undernourished or poorly nourished—if I may say so, with rickets, typhoid and worse. Today one sees a kind of school barracks in the vicinity, like those of the Waldorf School— barracks, not our present opulent building, but provisional barracks—except theirs are well and handsomely furnished. They are in a garden, but you need take only a few steps out of one of the gates and you'll be able to compare the people living in the most dreadful misery and dirt in the streets from which these children come with the way the children are turned out.

First of all the baths are exemplary. The children come at 8 a.m. and go home at night, so that they return to their homes every evening. In the mornings they first of all have a bath. Then comes a kind of school work, all of it with tremendous dedication, a touching sense of sacrifice, and everything organized in a practical way that is really touching. Miss McMillan also believes that Waldorf School education will have to be part of it all one day, and so one really has to say that from this point of view, too, we may regard that work with full satisfaction. One might perhaps wish to see some things done differently today where the methods are concerned, but in view of that sense of sacrifice this cannot be a consideration at present. Things are always evolving. And it is truly significant how well-behaved these children then are, especially at meal times when they are taken for their meals, serving themselves, with the food also always served by one of the children. What a practical approach can achieve is, for instance, evident in the fact that this heart-warming 'feeding' of the children, so nice one would really like to join them, comes to 2 shillings and 4 pence a head for the week. Everything is extraordinarily practical. It was really lovely, for example, how they then called together the older children, who have been at the centre for years, and they performed a long scene for us from Shakespeare's *A Midsummer Night's Dream*, showing real understanding and even a degree of stagecraft. It was moving, magnificent, how the children performed it, expressive and impressive, with real inner under-standing of dramatic art.

The performance of Shakespeare's *A Midsummer Night's Dream* was given almost in the same place where Shakespeare himself and his players once performed for the court. For the court of Queen Elizabeth I was near Greenwich then. The Queen's courtiers actually resided in the areas where the schoolrooms are today and also other rooms which I'll come to in a moment. There, outside London, Shakespeare had to perform his plays for the court. The children performed these scenes from Shakespeare's plays for us in the same place.

In the same area and connected with this education centre is a children's clinic, again for the poorest of the poor; 6,000 children are seen there in a year, not all at once, but through a year. Miss McMillan is also the head of this clinic. So in a very poor and underprivileged area, a dreadful area, someone is using all her energies and doing truly magnificent work.

It therefore gave me great satisfaction when Miss McMillan made known her intention first of all to visit our Waldorf School in Stuttgart with some of her teaching colleagues at Christmas. That body of teachers[43] is extraordinarily dedicated. You can imagine that caring for such children in the way I have just described is not exactly easy. And so it gave me great satisfaction that this very person took the chair for the Ilkley lectures and then in Penmaenmawr—where she came again for the few days she could manage—introduced the discussion on education in which Dr von Baravalle and Dr von Heydebrand took part. So everything that took place at Penmaen-mawr and in connection with it proved to be truly satisfactory.

The last, as it were, the third part were the days in London. Dr Wegman[44] had come to join me for the work I had to do in London. We had been asked to present the method and nature of our endeavours in anthroposophical medicine to a number of English physicians; 40 had been invited and most of them did also appear at Dr Larkins' house.[45] I was able to give two lectures,[46] speaking first about the particular nature of our medicines in connection with the symptoms and signs of diseases and the essential nature of the human being. In the second lecture I was able to provide a basis of a physiological and pathological kind for the functions of the human being, then something on the mode of action of individual medicines, again in connection with that basis—the actions of antimony, of mistletoe, and so on. I think we can truly say that the subject matter was met with quite good understanding also in a wider context, as evident from the fact that Dr Wegman was asked for a great number of consultations. It has therefore been possible to present this side of our anthroposophical work as well.

In conclusion we had a eurythmy performance at the Royal Academy of Art and it is fair to say that it proved extraordinarily successful. The hall is not particularly large, but it was not only sold out, people also had to be refused entry. The eurythmy was received with extraordinary enthusiasm. We can really say that eurythmy wins through wherever it goes. If only there were not those extraordinarily great obstacles today! On the one hand one sees all the positive responses, for instance the inclination shown by undertakings in Ilkley to have a kind of Waldorf School over there in England. But it is with great concern, and this is always with us today, that one sees the vague response, I'd say, painful in its effect, which comes when one asks oneself: 'What will become of the Waldorf School in a Germany which is in such dreadful danger, seeing that the endeavours in education have had their beginnings there?' I am not saying this so much because of the financial aspect but because of the extraordinarily endangered situation within Germany. There are things there where one has to say to oneself: 'If it goes on the way it does at the moment, one can hardly imagine how things will develop for the endeavours particularly concerning the Waldorf School.'

Ultimately, if things go on the way they are tending to go now, it will hardly be possible to take such things safely through the chaos of today. It is then with a heavy heart that one sees how these things exist after all, and all things in the world happen in a short-sighted way today, with people having no idea at all that spiritual streams must be involved in the development of our civilization, and that people far and wide have got out of the habit of taking an immediate interest in things and entering into them with gusto. Essentially everyone is asleep really when it comes to the things which are so dreadfully striking at the roots of human and earthly evolution. Humanity sleeps. At most people will moan about something that affects them directly. But things will not progress unless great ideas arise! The world is so unreceptive to the impulses that need to come in. People either do not want to hear or they feel uncomfortable in their world when reference is made to such things as for instance the dangerous situation in central Europe just now. They feel uncomfortable, do not like to talk about it, or add their own colour and rearrange things so that one will continue to speak of things that have no point to them, of guilt and the like. That is a way of keeping things at arm's length. It can be really painful today to see how people relate to events in the world at large. This general culture sleep, which is spreading more and more, is essentially something which is most pitiful. There is actually no awareness at all of how the earth and its civilization are a single whole today, even with such elementary events—I do not want to speak of them here and now but they have in fact happened—as the great tragedy in Japan,[47] a natural event that touches one deeply. If one considers how people would look at these things a relatively short time ago and how they look at them today, it is something which does again and again make one aware of the need to point out the urgent necessity for humanity to wake up.

This is, of course, something one is always aware of, especially when one sees once again what could be if people were to take an interest, taking things not according to regional or national divisions but in a general human sense. When one sees what could then be, and if on the other hand one sees how general sleepiness makes it almost impossible for anything to come about, this really does more than anything present the signature of our present age. That is the way things are—one cannot speak of just one thing without also getting the other picture for the given situation.

Today, my friends, I wanted to give you a kind of description of the trip. Tomorrow I will speak about issues concerning the spiritual life which are more removed from this and are really anthroposophical in content as a continuation.

My lecture will be at 8 o'clock tomorrow; there will be a eurythmy performance here at 8 o'clock on Tuesday.

Part Four

THE DRUID PRIEST'S SUN INITIATION AND HIS PERCEPTION OF THE MOON SPIRITS

LECTURE 5

FIRST of all I would remind you of some of the things I mentioned in the lectures on the spiritual nature of our planetary system which I gave here before I went away, going in more detail into the things to which I referred briefly yesterday. Reference had been made in a more spiritual sense to something you have known for a long time from what I wrote in my *Occult Science, an Outline*. We know that earth evolution is inwardly connected with the evolution of sun and moon. From many different points of view—the one considered in *Occult Science, an Outline* is but one of them—I pointed out that at a certain very early stage of our planetary system sun, moon and earth, and indeed the rest of the planets—though we won't go into that now—were a single whole and we must in a sense speak of the sun departing from, moving out of the whole—sun, moon, earth—with the moon then departing at a much later time.

All these things do, of course, have their outer aspect which derives from ideas based on the senses, as it were. But they do also have an inner aspect, which is that particular spirits are connected with either form of existence—sun existence and moon existence—spirits which had separated from that whole as the sun separated from the earth and gained an existence of a wholly different kind. For the subsequent evolution of earth we therefore cannot speak only of a separate sun having physical effects and etheric influences on the earth. When we also consider the spiritual aspect of the cosmos we must speak of a sun population, of sun spirits which were connected with earth evolution in the past and now are outside this earthly evolution, existing in a way that goes far beyond earthly existence and is much more sublime.

The same holds true for the moon population, as we may call them. In discussing the spiritual aspects of such cosmic events we also had to say that at one time an original wisdom existed within earth evolution. This did not, of course, consist of concepts flying about in the air but came from spirits which did not assume a physical body the way human beings do, but did nevertheless live in human beings because human beings had developed instinctive clairvoyant powers. The wisdom came from the spirits which continued their existence on the moon once the body of the moon had separated from the earth. As I said in that earlier lecture, therefore one has to say that within the moon entity—not in the sunlight reflected by the moon, nor in anything else which the moon reflects from the universe—within the inner part of this moon entity live the spirits which had once established the original wisdom among human beings on earth. Later these spirits entered into the myths, legends, the whole mythology, assuming the form of images which are no longer explicable to the ordinary human mind. These are elements of original wisdom which we look back on in wonder, though we only find them to be the true basis of the myths, legends, and so on, in an external way. The powers of today's human intellect will only fight their way through to that original wisdom with great effort by developing vision in images, inspiration and intuition again. However, something of an unconscious memory remained of all that was once bound up with the earth, at least within humanity itself. At different stages in the development of human civilization, and I am certainly including the earlier periods of civilization, these unconscious memories would then come up in human feeling, in the whole human state of soul. Looking at civilization in general, we may therefore speak of a sun-type and a moon-type civilization.

Those are memories coming to mind of something which did in earlier times work in human beings in a more comprehensive sense like forces of nature. And anything of which human beings were sentient in this respect was but like an adjunct, reminiscent of powers of growth or powers of internal organization.

If we now bring to mind what I have told you of my visit to England, we can pick up the thread of yesterday and, basing ourselves on the ideas we thus gained, enter a bit into the Druid culture of which I spoke yesterday more in its outer aspect. Traces of this are notably to be found in the regions where the lecture course of which I spoke yesterday was held.

The tools external science has available today will not answer the question as to the state of mind and soul in which these Druid priests lived. I could equally well call them Druid scholars, for these terms are entirely appropriate for those times, though of course they did not then have such terms. What lived in the impulses by means of which they guided their congregation?

In history we often hear something which we hear only too often, and it always merely signifies something which was astir in times of decline, of decadence. Here I want to speak of something which always relates to something which came before these periods of decline, something alive in the flowering period. For these cromlechs,* these sun circles, of which I spoke yesterday, do very much remind us in what they truly are of the way things were there when the Druid mysteries were in their flowering period. Using the means which anthroposophical spiritual science puts at our disposal we can even today enter into the way in which those Druid priests served their people. In a way they were everything to their people, or rather their tribes. They provided for the people's religious needs—in so far as one can speak of such in those earlier times. They were the authority for the social impulses. They also determined the healing method of that time. They united in themselves all the things which later were divided up among many branches of civilized human life.

---

* The term 'cromlech' has two meanings—grave chamber and circle of standing stones. Today it refers mainly to grave chambers in the British Isles, and to stone circles, or standing stones, in Brittany.

The only way of looking at this Druid culture—which is what we may indeed call it—is to consider the important aspects of it in a period that came before the one from which those mythological ideas echo across to us from the north, the mythologies connected with the name Woden or Odin. The aspects connected with the name Woden essentially belong to a time which came after this period when Druid culture was in flower. In the circle of wisdom, we might say, which points to the name Woden or Odin we have to see something of a circle of wisdom which initially came from the East, from a mystery circle located in the region of the Black Sea. This then poured its spiritual content from East to West, with mystery centres established in many different ways as colonies, in a way, all the way from the Black Sea to the West.

All of it shone into a sublime culture, sublime in a deeper sense, into original wisdom, Druid wisdom. The wisdom of the Druids was in fact an unconscious echo, something of an unconscious memory of everything which the earth had received from sun and moon before sun and moon separated from it. In the Druid mysteries, initiation was essentially a sun initiation and connected with the element which through sun initiation would then become moon wisdom. What was the real intention behind these cromlechs, these Druid circles? From what I said yesterday you will realize that essentially they were intended for the study of the relationship between earth and sun. Looking at the individual sites we find that they are really some kind of instrument used to cut out the external, physical effects of the sun. The initiate, with the gift of a seer, would then be able to observe such sun influences as remained in the area of darkness. With the aid of the cromlechs the Druid priest observed the inner qualities of the sun's light and how they were reflected back into the cosmos from the earth. I would therefore like to say that the physical nature of the sun's light was held off. As I told you yesterday, a dark space was created by placing the stones in the ground and a covering stone on top. With the power of seeing through the stones it was then possible to observe the spiritual essence of the sun's light in that dark space.

So the Druid priest, standing before his altar, would be considering the inner qualities of sun nature in so far as he needed what would flow into him there, full of wisdom—but it flowed into him in such a way that the wisdom was still like a force of nature. The priest would consider the things he needed to govern his congregation.

You must understand, of course, that we are speaking of a time when you could not look in the calendar to know when one must sow in the right way, when one should entrust this or that seed grain to the soil. Their calendar was something which the priest read in the sun effects. People did not pick up a book to inform themselves about time. The only book available was the universe itself. And the letters which made up the words came from observations as to how the sun influenced one thing or another that had been set up as a device. Today, if you want to know something you look it up in a book. Then the Druid priest would look to see what the sun was doing at his cromlechs. There he would read the secrets of the universe. He would know when wheat, rye and so on should be sown from what he read there. These are just examples. The priest would read the impulses that came from the universe for everything that was done in those days. The major impulses needed to complete the calendar for the year came from observations made in the shadow cast in the Druid circle. In those days, therefore, when there was nothing that had come from human intellect, the universe itself was one and all. Instead of printing presses they had the cromlechs, to coax the secrets out from the universe.

Reading the cosmic book in this way, as it were, one was working with sun nature, sun quality. And they were sentient of moon nature or moon quality being the opposite of sun quality. The powers that had concentrated in the moon at that time had once been connected with the earth.

They did not depart completely, however, for they left something behind them in the earth. If there were only sun powers, then only proliferating, growing cells would develop; for instance, all life would always arise with small or large cell character. Variety, with things configured out, does not come from the sun powers but from the moon powers that work together with the sun powers.

The situation was that when the Druid priest exposed himself to whatever his circles, his cromlechs, would yield he did not only get the abstract impression which we do quite rightly get today when we concern ourselves intellectually with things of the spirit. The powers of the sun would speak directly to the priest. The spiritual sun quality would have an immediate influence in the shadow cast by the sun and would influence him with much greater intensity than a sensory perception does on us today, for much more profound powers were involved. The priest would stand before his ritual site and observe this sun quality. As he did so his breathing would change, growing lifeless, blunted, wavering, so that one breath would merge into the next. With the part of himself which as a human being he was thanks to his breathing the priest would live in the sun influence he encountered there. This did not give him abstract knowledge but something which acted in him the way the blood circulation acts, inwardly pulsing through him, stirring up his human nature even at the physical level. But this influence which went as far as the physical aspect did also have a spiritual part. It was the inner stirrings that he experienced that actually were his knowledge.

We have to think of this knowledge in a much more living, intensive way as living experience. The priest would also only gain such knowledge at particular times. It could be aroused at every noon tide, but in reduced strength. But when it was a question of the major secrets being revealed, the priest had to expose himself to these influences at the time that we call St John's Tide today. Then the great wave would join the small waves of his knowledge that came daily. Experiencing the sun influences in this special, artistic way on earth, the priest felt this to be his initiation, the sun initiation, and this enabled him to study and understand the powers left behind as moon powers when the moon separated from the earth. That would then be his knowledge of nature, gained under the influence of his sun initiation. Anything revealed to him on the surface of things was not important to him. The moon powers of the earth which billowed up from below, they were important to him. Through the initiation principle, traces of which still remain even today in these memorials, the priest gained the power of insight, and he would perceive what is at work in nature particularly when the night sky let the stars emerge above the earth and the moon moved through the heavens.

The sun initiation gave him the spiritual aspect, the spiritual impulse, and this gave him his knowledge of nature. His natural science was a moon science. He was sentient of the moon powers that were behind this. Shining up from the depths of the earth in the plants, they were active in wind and weather and the other elements. He would be sentient of these, sentient not in the abstract way in which we are sentient of the forces of nature with our earthly science today. He would be sentient of them as very much active and alive, such being their nature.

In the living experience gained there, the priest would be sentient of these being the elemental spirits which lived in the plants, in the stones, in everything. These elemental spirits, their dwelling places being in the trees, in the plants and so on, were kept within limits, but those limits were not as narrow as those set for human beings today, for instance—they were wider. This is how the Druid priest with his moon science of nature was able to see how these elemental spirits could grow to their full size, turning into giants.

This led to perception of the giants known as the Jötnar. Looking into the root sphere of a plant underground, where moon nature lived, one would see the elemental within its proper limits [drawing on the board; *Tafel* (Plate) 7 in *Wandtafelzeichnungen* vol. XIII]. But those elementals were wanting to go forth and grow outwardly to giant size. When the elementals of this type, which brought such benefit to the root region, grew out into giants they turned into the frost giant, with the frost their outer symbol. They lived in everything that moves across the earth as destructive hoar frost or other kinds of devastating frosts. Root powers of plants let loose lived in frost and hoar and in everything that passed across the earth in giant strides with devastating effect. Yet in the root sphere they were of great benefit. The element of leaf growth could also grow to giant size. It would then live as elemental spirit magnified to giant size in the drifting fogs or mists that passed across the earth with everything it contained at certain times of the year, bearing the pollen of plants and so forth. And when the principle which lives in a gentle, modest way in the flowering powers of plants grows to giant size it turns into devastating fire.

Meteorological events were thus seen as elemental powers, which in the natural world lived within their proper limit, having grown to giant size. The very sites chosen for these ancient pagan places of worship show that the things which on the one hand were given through sun circles and dolmen were then developed further in the earthly insight and perception they had made possible—developed in such a way that one was able to observe in the right way the mysterious movements and activities, flow and life of wind and weather, the way the elements of water and air, the hoar frost welling forth from the soil, and the dew worked together. Sun initiation and moon spirit insight thus gave rise to that most ancient idea which, I'd like to say, we find to be part of the basis of European civilization.

The Druid priest would thus read anything his devices and his sun initiation permitted him to read from the cosmos, and the knowledge he was then—stimulated by this sun initiation—able to gain from his moon science. The whole of social and religious life was also bound up with this. For the things the priest was able to say to people were something which extended to the spiritual basis of the world in which they were. It is easiest to see this if one considers the healing knowledge which the priests had. On the one hand they would see the elemental spirits held within their limits in the various things to be found in the mineral world, the plant world and so on. They would observe what happened with plants when these were exposed to frost, let us say, when they were exposed to the forces which the storm giants, the wind giants carry through the air, when they were exposed to the boiling heat of the fire giants. In studying what the hoar frost giants, the frost giants, the storm giants, the fire giants would do to plants if let loose they found their own way of taking plants and within limits imitate the effects that the giants achieved in nature—to subject plants to a specific process, such a freezing, cooling, combustion, dissolving and binding.

The Druid priests would say to themselves: 'Looking into the natural world we see the devastating actions of the frost giants, the storm giants, the fire giants. But we can take what these giants, these Jötnar, spread about the world in their ungainly way; we can take this away from them. We can confine these moon powers that have been let loose within narrower limits again.'

They produced their medicines, healing herbs and so on, by studying and making use of the things that happened when the soil was thawing, what happened in a storm, in the wind, in the boiling heat of the sun, applying the same principles to the sun quality that lived in the plants and which they had received with their initiation. Those medicines were based on the giants being reconciled with the gods.

In those days every medicine bore witness to the reconciliation between the enemies of the gods and the gods themselves. Foods were taken in under the immediate sun and moon influence, as nature offered them. A medicine was produced by a human being who would take the things nature did further, taming the power of giants to make it serve the power of the sun.

You see this whole way of living is only thinkable if there is no intellectualized inner knowledge, not a trace of it, when everything one wants to know is perceived as spirit coming to expression in the phenomena of nature themselves or in what can be learned from natural phenomena with the initiation principle, using special devices, when everything is read in the book of the cosmos itself. Only then is such a life, such a kind of civilization possible.

We have to think of this civilization as spread out across large parts of northern and central Europe about three or three and a half millennia ago. Nothing existed then that was similar to writing. Only this cosmic script existed. And coming from the East, initially from a mystery centre in the region of the Black Sea, something spread there which our ordinary mind can no longer grasp, which is now to be found in the Norse mythology which relates to Woden.

What actually is Woden? The mystery from which this Woden culture arose was a mystery of Mercury, a mystery which added the impulses of Mercury to those of sun and moon. We might say that this ancient culture was in a state of innocence and naivety in the lustre of sun and moon, untouched by the things that could be told to humanity through the Mercury impulses. These existed only over in the East at that time. From there they spread to the West, colonizing. Woden-Mercury spread his influence to the West.

This also casts a light on the way in which Woden is said to have brought the skill of runes, the writing in runes. He was therefore seen as the giver of what human beings brought forth themselves as the skill of deciphering the universe, initially in a very primitive intellectualistic way. That was the first intellectualistic element, the Woden element. So we may say that Mercury quality, Woden quality had been added to sun and moon quality.

Where this Woden element really entered as a full impulse, it would have an influence on all earlier experiences. Everything was in a way tinged, given a certain impulse coming from this Woden quality. For there was one particular secret of Druid culture. Things will of course germinate, come up everywhere, even in places where they do not belong; weeds also grow in the fields. In Druid civilization, only sun and moon qualities were considered 'good herbage' of their culture. If it happened that the intellectualistic principle came up ahead of time, then it would be considered a 'weed'. Among the many different medicines which the Druids had was also one to treat brooding, the Mercury quality. It may seem paradoxical to people today, but they had a remedy for broodiness, for getting wrapped up in one's own inner life, the state of one's own soul. The Druids wanted people to live with nature, not getting wrapped up in themselves. They considered someone sick even if he merely tried somehow to reflect nature in a primitive art, except perhaps by imitating it, or if he tried to produce signs. Someone who produced signs was sick and had to be cured. Such a person would then be considered to be a black soul, not a white one. Indeed, if we, in our present state of knowledge, had been transported into Druid civilization we would all have ended up in hospital being cured!

And then the Woden civilization[48] brought this disease across from the East. It was felt to be a disease, this Woden civilization. It brought the element which earlier on had presented only as an abnormal broodiness, but now with a force that had itself grown enormous, gigantic. This is what it brought. It brought the rune into something that before had only been learned from the cosmic script. It made people put their intellectualistic powers into the sign, it brought everything which was felt to be Mercury culture. No wonder then that something which came from this Woden culture, which was felt to be like something separated out from its best powers, the Baldur spirit,[49] the late-born sun spirit, could not be seen together with life but only with death. Baldur had to go to Hel, into the dark powers of death, into the dwelling place of death.

And again, something to which people had initially given the most thought—as evident still from the Edda traditions[50]—was not how to free Baldur, this son of the Woden powers, from Hel—that was really only a later idea—but how to heal him. And the way this came out was that they said they had many remedies, but there was no medicine for Baldur, for the intelligence arising from Woden's rune power must inevitably lead to death.

Thus we see something again to which I have drawn your attention from different points of view before when considering human evolution. In earlier times human beings had instinctive insight and knew nothing of the significance of death. They remembered life before coming to earth and knew that death is merely a change to a different condition. Death was not felt to be any kind of major hiatus. Above all death was not a tragedy in earlier times. It only became one as the Mystery on Golgotha approached, and this brought the redemption from fear of death. In the Baldur legend you have an excellent illustration of how the arrival of intellectualism created the state of soul where one takes death into account. So that is how this entered into human evolution. The death of Baldur, who could not rise again, could be healed again only in soul and spirit when there was also the Christ figure, who could rise again from death.

It is truly marvellous how up there in the North the influence of the powers of Mercury on those of sun and moon paved the way for the view of the Christ impulse. We see Baldur, the god who is subject to death and cannot rise again, as the forerunner of the Christ who also became subject to death but was able to rise again. This was because the Christ was coming directly from the sun. Baldur, coming from Woden as the sun's power, was power of sun reflected by Mercury, sun power shining out in the runes, sun power out of the signs which human beings made using their intellect.

We see how everything evolved in those northern regions, evolved clearly for us to see, for there we still see the human being as he lived, reading in the cosmos, searching the cosmos for religious, social and healing ideas. Later humanity came to dwell with the earth's powers. The Druid priest would stand by his sacrificial stone and look to see how the sun's shadow took shape, with the spiritual aspect of the sun evident in the shadow; this he would read. Later came the time when essential sun nature, captured as it were in the dolmens, the crom-lechs, was drawn in abstract lines called rays—a dreadful thing to say when a higher view is taken. And we approach the time when the relationship of the life in root and leaf and flower with the life in frost, wind and fire was only seen in chemical terms. The giants and the elemental spirits have changed into forces of nature. Yet the forces of nature contain nothing but those giants of old; it is just that people do not realize this and feel enormously superior. The forces of nature have evolved in a straight line from the giants; they are the late-born offspring. Today we live in a culture that is wholly derivative. When the eye is directed to those wholly dilapidated remnants of Druid times, we must really feel deeply touched. It is as if we were looking at the distant ancestry of our present-day life.

Let us go into some detail. Today we speak in a strangely abstract way also of medicines, very intellectualistically, describing the methods of manufacture in a completely abstract way. We have to think of it transformed into something full of life if we want to look back on the way in which the Druid priest considered his medicines. He would be sentient of the sun powers, with which he was familiar, and which he treated in plants and other products of nature using the powers of the giants. This was wholly alive to him. He elicited the powers for transforming the plant into a medicament from the giants. He knew that with this, he was doing something for the whole cosmos. And he would then look at the human being. His special insight into human nature allowed him to see how with the dream images that came, an indefinite, unconscious flickering up of deeper human nature, dawning awareness, those things had their actions under the means of taming the giants' powers which had been placed in the inner human being. On the one hand he had his Loki[51] out there in the wild conflagrations, and on the other hand he had the principles he had taken from Loki that allowed him to transform one plant or another in a combustion process. The way in which this took effect within the human being would show him the Loki power within the human being. It had been disarmed. And he would say to himself: 'When something which can mean devastation, a threatening danger out there in the world of the giants, is introduced into the inner human being in the right way, then it will heal.' The powers which poisons have on the large scale can be healing if taken to the right place.

The priest thus had his own way of gaining insight into nature's different powers, forces and modes of action. He had entered into the spirit and, thanks to this, sent religious, social, medical and other impulses out into his congregation. The initiates of those early times thus preserved the ancient wisdom that the moon spirits had cultivated for as long as they themselves were still on earth. The wisdom was no longer immediately available when the moon spirits had departed with the moon. But the initiates explored and established it with the help of a kind of sun initiation in the way that I have described to you today.

Part Five

THE PAST, PRESENT AND FUTURE
DEVELOPMENT OF THE HUMAN MIND

LECTURE 6

The subject for the lectures I am going to give at this conference will be essential human nature as it has evolved, developed at a particular time in the past, as it is in the immediate present and what the prospects for it are in future human evolution on planet earth. With every promising philosophy of life that has flowed into western civilization with its American appendage, the aim has been not only to consider the human being in the present age of humanity, pointing out how the individual appears in his place within the whole of humanity on earth, but it has been a feature of the very philosophies which were likely to be accepted into occidental civilization that the human being was always also seen in the historical evolution of humanity on earth, bringing the present-day human being together with the human being of the past either up to a certain point, as in the Old Testament, or more as earthly history, or also higher up—including a study of planetary evolutions in the cosmos. This was not so much a feature of oriental philosophies nor of the earlier philosophies in Europe, in so far as they were not yet part of modern civilization. They limited themselves more to placing the human being in the given space, as it were. Because of the way we have been brought up, being part of occidental evolution, our sentience, our feelings, could not be satisfied with merely placing man in the world's physical space. We have a certain inner instinct which demands that we are together with our brothers, as it were, not only with the people of the present time in physical space but also with the people of earlier times, for it is only together with the people of today and those of the future that they make up the whole human race. We will not gain a satisfactory view on this historical evolution of man in the narrower or wider sense if we consider only the external anthropological evidence. External documents, however cleverly interpreted, cannot encompass the evolution of man, for man has body, mind or soul, and spirit. The spirit has always shone through man to a greater or lesser degree so that conscious awareness has been living in him. And the evolution of the human mind really shows itself to be such that one can see the whole essence and nature of man in this unfolding of the mind, just as with our senses we are ultimately able to perceive the nature of the plant in its flower.

Let us therefore consider this, the most important element in human evolution, the evolution of the human mind. If we look at the human mind today we find that we can make the following distinction. In the ordinary waking state in which we are from waking up until going to sleep, we develop a more or less clear, bright ability to form ideas. This grows from the depths of the life of feeling as a flower does from the plant. Compared to the clear bright life of ideas, the life of feeling is like something that is more or less half unconscious, dark, inwardly billowing and moving, and never being really entirely clear. Deeper down than our feelings, which do at least also give very direct impulses to our life in ideas, much further down are then the will impulses. I have quite often spoken to anthroposophists that when it comes to the will impulses human beings are essentially asleep even in their waking hours. The principle that lives in the will impulses in the human being himself really does not at all come to conscious awareness in today's waking state. We have a notion that we are going to do one thing or another. That is not yet the will impulse; within it lies the intention to have a will impulse, taking the form of an idea. The principle represented by this intention then goes deep down into our essential human nature, into depths that have no greater clarity for the mind than dreamless sleep. And it rises up again as will impulse, rises up in what our arms and hands, our legs, our feet are doing, things we do with the objects of the outside world. The things we thus do from will impulses in our own body, the changes we make to the outside world through our will impulses come to conscious awareness because we form ideas, ideas also connected with feelings. In our ordinary state of consciousness we have only the beginning and the end of the will impulse, the intention as an idea, and the observation of moving ourselves or moving things in the outside world as the consequence of our intentions. Anything in between—how our soul's intentions pour into the organism, how the soul stimulates body warmth, movement of the blood, of muscle and so on in order to become will impulse—all this remains as unconscious as do the elements of dreamless sleep. For it simply is the case that someone who is truly able to observe his experiences has to say to himself, 'I am really only awake when forming ideas. I dream in my feelings; I sleep in my will impulses.' And it really is nothing else with these will impulses but what happens when we wake up in the morning and realize that our organism has restored and refreshed itself in a particular way. We perceive the experiences of sleep as we wake up, we intend to do this or that, we also send our intentions unconsciously down into our organism; their life is a life of sleep when they change into actions, and we only wake up again when we act and see the results of what has been going on inside us but has been at an unconscious level.

Those are the major elements, as it were, of human inner experience when awake, when dreaming, when asleep. For the dreams we have at night, in sleep, have little connection with our life in ideas. They follow laws that differ completely from the logical laws of our life in ideas. Yet one is able to observe, if one goes into things, if one is able to do that, one will find that the course taken by dreams, this marvellous dramatic progress they often follow, shows extraordinary similarity to our life in feelings. If we were able only to feel when awake, the feelings themselves would not be similar to the dream images, but their inner drama, tensions, relief, wish impulses, disasters of inner experiences that may wallow in feelings—they present to our feeling with all the 'lack of definition' or if you like definition one also gets with dreams, except that a dream lives in images, and our life of feeling in the characteristic experiences which we identify with terms of inner sentience in feeling. We may therefore see feeling and our actual dreaming as dream states in the present-day human mind, and the processes of will impulses and those of actual dreamless sleep as belonging to the present-day human being's sleep level of consciousness.

We have to understand that the basic aspects of the conscious mind as it is today have not that long ago also gone through a process of development, a development which people prefer not to speak of in our present materialistic age. Yet we will no longer understand things that have come down to us as documents of human thought as early as the first Christian centuries unless we are aware that something very different lived in the inner human being when he was thinking than lives in the inner soul today. And there is need to point out that it is downright ignorance in our souls to approach a work such as John Scotus Erigena's *Periphyseon* [*De divisione naturae* or 'the division of nature'], written in the ninth century,[53] let us say with the kind of life of ideas we have been brought up in, or the old books on alchemy. Today's way of thinking does not allow us to understand what was meant at that time. You read words and do not understand what people meant by them. From the fifteenth century onwards, human thinking has borne a quite specific stamp, and although this developed slowly and gradually it has, relatively speaking, already reached its high point today. This form of thinking, being the actual waking state in present-day human life, as I have shown, is really such that essentially present-day people cannot find happiness. People think that only their waking experiences have light and clarity; they think it is the only thing by means of which, drawing on their inner life, they also compose the most marvellous results in the sciences. Essentially, however, people do not find happiness at all with this present way of thinking to meet their inner longings. For they actually lose themselves in this present-day thinking. They lose themselves so that this thinking is the only clear content of the mind, much clearer than the blood circulation, for instance, or their breathing. Those remain dark and unclear in lower regions of the conscious mind. One feels that a reality lives in them, but one really sleeps through this reality and is awake only in forming ideas, in thinking. But particularly if one is a bit inclined, let us say, to practise self-reflection, one will find, 'You are actually losing yourself in the thinking which is really the only thing you have in your inner life.' And there are two connections, I would say—this is, of course, meant to be a mental image—where this losing oneself in thought becomes quite tangible.

A thinker of more recent times, Descartes,[54] coined the modern phrase *Cogito ergo sum*, 'I think, therefore I am.' Yes, those are the words of a philosopher. But people of more recent times do not say so, are unable to say so. They say, 'When I merely think something, experience it in thought, it simply *is* not, and when I think myself, surely I *am* not—such thoughts are at most images; it is the most certain thing in me, but I do not take hold of existence in my thinking.' People also say that something one is merely thinking is but a thought. Descartes therefore is desperately insisting: 'One would wish to be, and nowhere else are there points of reference where we can grasp this being, this existence, of man in the thinking of more recent times. One is therefore looking for it in the very place where according to general sentience it definitely is not—in one's thinking.' Every sleep negates Descartes' words. We do not think in our sleep. Is it that then we *are* not? Do we die at night and are born again in the mornings? Or *are* we, do we exist, from going to sleep to waking up? The simplest truths do not take account of the views currently held in the world. Those words reflect a desperate clinging to something with one's being, 'I think, therefore I am,' and not any kind of inner experience. So that is one thing.

The other connection we may refer to is this. Apart from our thinking, and modern people are very proud of it, we also have the findings of modern natural science, of observations, and the results of experiments. Well, yes, but the way they are is that they do not allow us to look into the actual being or existence of things but only in the changes they undergo, into ephemera. In spite of this, modern man finds that a thought is only justifiable if it has been taken from this external kind of existence which, however, only shows itself in its outer revelation. Modern man has therefore stopped altogether to grasp his existence in himself. Thinking is much too airy for this. But anything else that is within him he will at most find in the way in which the external realms of nature are found in the natural sciences. And that is where modern man then looks for reality, existence. And he believes in himself only in so far as he is nature. As a result nature with its reality becomes the Moloch, the god demanding human sacrifice, who is really depriving modern man of his sense of reality, of being in existence. There will no doubt be many people who say that they do not feel any of this, that it is not so. But that is just one opinion. The feelings of people today, those who are even just beginning to practise a bit of self-reflection, really arise wholly from the mood I have been describing. Modern man is encapsulated in this kind of experience of his own essential nature and his relationship to the surrounding world. He then applies the things he discovers in that encapsulation to his awareness of the world, looking at the stars through his instruments, for instance, the spectroscope, the telescope. He notes down what he sees there and makes it into a purely spatial astronomy, astrophysics and so on. He does not realize that he has actually just taken up to the heavens something which he has observed and calculated in and for things on earth.

If I have a source of light here, everyone will agree that when I have gone many thousand miles away from that light source the light out there in space will have grown weak, or may perhaps no longer be visible. Everyone knows that the luminosity of the light decreases with distance. A law of physics also says that gravity decreases to the square of the distance. Yet people do not take the thought any further. That gravity has a certain value here on earth and decreases to the square of the distance is something people understand because we live here on earth, establish laws of nature, fathom earth truths and connect them. They are true where gravity has a particular value. Gravity decreases and so do the truths. Something that holds true on earth ceases to be true as we follow its spread in the cosmos. We do not have the right to apply the physics and chemistry we establish here on earth in simple analogy, just as we cannot apply the values for gravity on earth and in its immediate surroundings to the cosmos. We must not consider the truth that pertains to the spheres of heaven to be the same as the truth we know here on earth. We know that this is something enormously paradoxical, indeed fantastic, for modern people to hear. But that is how it is at the present time. The encapsulation of general conscious awareness has grown so powerful that a paradox must result as soon as we make the least pinprick in the capsule with something we say. It is in connection with all these things that human beings are really completely bound to the earth today, so that none of their insights and often not even their reflections can go beyond the things they experience on earth. And they do the same thing with cosmic time as they do with cosmic space.

You see—I have often been discussing these particular truths in anthroposophical circles and what I am going to say now is repeating this, using a single example—this was particularly evident when I was invited by our English anthroposophical friends to give a course of lectures in Penmaenmawr in the second half of August.[55] This is in Wales, where Anglesey island lies near the west coast of Britain. It is indeed a quite remarkable region, a region which shows that there really are also geographies all over the globe which differ from those found in ordinary schoolbooks, even the schoolbooks at a higher level. People consider it quite advanced today to include the nature of the vegetation, the fauna and flora when describing the geography of a place, and still base themselves on the geology, palaeontology of the rocks, and so on. But there are much more inward differentiations across the globe than those commonly used for the geology of our earth. In Penmaenmawr, where the lecture course was given, you take a few steps, as it were, one to one and a half hours into the mountains, and you'll everywhere find the remnants of the ancient Druid rites—decayed stone structures of a simple kind. Thus stones have been put together to enclose something of a small chamber, with a covering stone. There sunlight was excluded in a makeshift way, so that it would be dark inside. It cannot be denied that those cromlechs also served as burial places, for the most important ritual sites have always been built above the graves of others. Here, however, we have something entirely different as well, also with these simple cromlechs, and this is evident from what are called the Druid circles. It was really very beautiful to see, when I went up one such mountain near Penmaenmawr where the sparse remnants of two Druid circles may still be seen today, lying close together. The stones were positioned in such a way that one can see today that there have once been twelve of them. And someone who wants to see what this was all about will look and see that what mattered was this. As the sun followed its course in the cosmos, be it in the course of a day, be it in the course of a year, it would always cast its shadow in a particular way—one way of one stone, another of another. Watching how the shadow changed in the course of the day or the year, one was able to follow the course of the sun.

People are sensitive to light today, particularly if the light is also bearing warmth, or the warmth is bearing light. Even today, human minds register the difference between sunlight in summer and sunlight in winter, because one feels hot in summer and cold in winter. People also note more subtle differences. But the differences in the light that one notes because one is cold or hot can also be seen in the shadow. It is not the same if it is the October, July or August sun which casts the shadow, not only where the direction is concerned but also in inner quality. It was one of the tasks of the Druid priest to be able to perceive the quality of the shadow, that strange addition, one might say, of a reddish tone to the August shadow, a bluish tone to the November or December shadow. Their training enabled the Druid priests to read the daily path of the sun in the shadow. They could read the annual path of the sun in the shadow. It is still evident from these remnants today that one of the tasks undertaken there was of that nature. Many other things were part of the ritual, a sun worship that was not some kind of abstraction, not even the abstraction of mere devotion and humility. It would be absolutely wrong to think so, though this is no reason to underestimate devotion and humility. But here it was not abstract devotions and abstract humility which mattered, but there was something else as well to the ritual.

You see, the grain of wheat, the seed of rye needs to be buried in the ground at a specific time of the year. It is not good if they are put in the ground at the wrong time. Someone who knows these things very well will know that it matters if seed is sown a few days sooner or later. And there are also other things in human life. The life of the people who once lived in the geographical area where the Druids performed their rites, perhaps three millennia ago—life was no doubt extraordinarily simple, with agriculture and animal husbandry the main activities. But let us ask ourselves, how were they to know when to sow and to harvest in the right way, when many other things needed to be done which were connected with developments in the natural world through the year? People will say that today country people have their farmers' calendars which tell them that this is the day for doing such and such, and this the day for such and such. These things are quite brilliant. Yes, we are living in an age when the human mind is such that these things are recorded and one can read them in print. It does not occur to one that one is getting them from the printed page, but that is how it is. But at the time when Druid worship was at its height people did not have anything like this, not even the most primitive beginnings of reading and writing. But what they did have was that the priest could stand in such a Druid circle and observe its shadows. According to the shadow he would say that for the next week the countryman should do this or that, the bull has to be taken through the herd, for that will be the right time for servicing the cows. People read in the cosmos and had the device that allowed them to do so. They would stand on the earth, and in order to do what needed to be done on earth they would read what the sun itself told in the signs produced in those stone circles of which only sparse remnants remain.

That was a very different state of the human soul and it would be serious arrogance of people today who can read and write a bit to underestimate the art involved in establishing the actions and devices thanks to such heavenly revelation. I would say that in those sites one is compelled to recall also many other things which spiritual science permits us to investigate. I have on various occasions said among anthroposophists that everything which needs to be investigated using spiritual science cannot really be thought in ordinary thoughts. We have to think in images. I hope you all know what I have said about images, imaginations, in my book *Knowledge of the Higher Worlds*. This was disputed this morning, but I think that it does not apply to those present. One must always have these visions in images in the soul when speaking of something observed directly in the spirit and not with the physical senses. The actual spiritual-scientific descriptions given from this place here or in the Landhausstrasse in Stuttgart[56] were based on such imaginations. But they are much more alive than are mere abstract thoughts. It simply is the nature of abstract thoughts that one grasps not a trace of reality but only images of reality in such thoughts. You touch and feel imaginations with your active thinking, just as you would touch and feel tables and chairs. When one gains insight not in abstract concepts but in imaginations one is filled with reality, existence, in a much more robust way. Someone speaking out of imaginations always has them before him as if he were writing them down. But this is not writing with those cruelly abstract letters we use in writing but in cosmic images.

Well now, how is it with these imaginations in our region? Those who are familiar with it will know that it is relatively easy to arrive at these imaginations here, that they are relatively easy to produce. If one is conscientious, aware of one's responsibility (which one must always be aware of when saying anything at all that comes from spiritual science), one will of course also allow such an imagination to stand, that is, write it down in the spirit—for uttering them is merely the uttering of what is written—if one has turned it over many times, has tested and checked it many times over. Speaking out of the spiritual world with a full sense of responsibility does not make the words come easily from one's lips. Yet is is possible to say that in regions such as ours such imaginations are written down with relative ease, but they will just as easily erase themselves. For someone who produces spiritual subject matter in imaginations—one cannot call it anything else—in our region it is as if you write and then immediately erase what has been written; it is quickly erased. In that other region, where sea and land meet, ebb and flood come every day, where the wind goes right through you—we not only felt the wind come in through the window in the hotel where we stayed on the ground floor, but we walked across the carpet as if on the billows of the sea, with the wind passing through underneath the carpet—it did really go right through one, and the whole of nature there is so much astir, joyfully stirred, that cloudbursts often alternate with sunshine hour by hour. There you are in a natural world full of joyful life and literally cannot help yourself but then also remember how this natural world revealed itself to the Druid priests of old—I might also call them Druid scholars, it is one and the same thing—when they looked down on it from their elevated seat. What did the earth look like to the Druid priests' inner eye, since the heavens appeared to be as I have just described?

It is most interesting to observe. But one only arrives at the complete memory if one now understands the particular geographical differentiation in that place. There it takes a much greater effort to create the imaginations, much more than here, for instance. They do not easily inscribe themselves in the astral atmosphere, as it were. But they persist for a long time, are fixed, do not erase so quickly. We now come to see why the Druid priests sought out those particular places for their rites, for their more important rites, where the spiritual principle approaching the human being has marked features thanks to the nature of the place. Those very Druid circles which we visited there, if one had moved up into the air in a balloon, looking down from above on the smaller and the larger circle—they were at some distance, but if one was high enough it would not have been so apparent—the two circles would have looked like the ground plan of the burned-down Goetheanum. It is most beautifully situated!

As you walk up the mountain there are many places from where you have great views of mountain and sea. Then you reach the top. These Druid circles are in a large depression in the mountain so that you find yourself surrounded by mountains, and the Druid circles are in this depression. That is where the Druid priest would look for wisdom, as he knew it, for knowledge and insight. That is where he looked for his sun wisdom and also wisdom relating to nature. Having thus entered into the whole complex of what existed on earth and what came down from heaven, the priest found something very different in the growth of plants, the growth of all vegetation from what it has come to be to people of later times, people who thought in abstracts. When sun nature has been grasped by considering on the one hand the sense-perceptible rays of the sun which enter into the eye and on the other hand the shadow with its many differentiations, then you know that the spiritual sun lives on in the differentiation of the shadow. Shadow cast on other bodies only keeps away the physical side of the sun's rays; the spiritual side comes through. In the cromlechs, as described, was a dark inner space that had been closed off in a makeshift way. Only the physical sunlight does not enter, but the influences do enter, and thanks to these influences the Druid priest grew into a state of being inwardly filled with the secret powers of cosmic existence, into the secrets of the world. He came to see, for instance, the work which the sun did on the plant. He would see how this plant thrives at this time of the year, when the sun's influence is of a particular kind. He followed the sun in its spirituality, how it flows, pours into flower, leaf, root and so on. He followed the influence of the sun as it was or is on animals. Being able to gain inner insight into the sun's actions in this aspect, he also came to see how other influences in the cosmos, like the moon influences, for example, poured into those sun influences. He then said to himself, 'The sun's influence on the plant brings shooting, sprouting life, something that wants to go on and on.' The Druid priest knew that when a plant growing from the soil was exposed only to the sun it would grow to infinity. The sun wants shooting, sprouting life. It is due to the moon influences, which are not only in the sunlight reflected back from the moon, that this life is held up, configured, that leaves, flower, fruit and seed assume a specific form, that the striving for infinity is set many kinds of limits. The moon reflects all influences, and these are given off in the quality that grows upwards from the root, lives in animal reproduction and so forth.

Let us take a particular case. The Druid priest looked at the growing plant. He saw how the plant grew, he saw in a living way the principle that Goethe was to follow later in a more abstract way in his *Metamorphosis*.[57] He would see the sun powers streaming down, and also the reflected powers of the sun in the element that configures the plant; in his natural science he saw sun and moon working together in every single plant, every single animal. He knew what sun and moon did to the root, which is still down in the ground and has to depend on absorbing the salts of the earth in a particular way. Sun and moon do something very different in the leaf, which comes away from the ground and stretches out into the air. And he would see something else again in the flower, which comes away from the earth and strives towards the light, the light of the sun. He would see them as one, sun influence and moon influence, mediated through the earth's influence. Plant growth, animal nature, he would see it all together in one. He was of course living there in the way in which we also did live there, with stormy winds all around which tell one so much of the configuration of the region, of those peculiar beautiful gifts of the weather that are full of life. On one occasion, when a eurythmy performance started in a hall built of wood, people were sitting under their umbrellas because a cloudburst had immediately preceded the event and was still continuing when the eurythmy started. The curtains were getting quite wet. Being so closely bound up with the weather is something you can still experience very well in that place, and the Druid priest did as well, of course. Nature was not so stand-offish, it embraced one then and still does so today. You are, I'd say— truly, it is something extraordinarily nice—almost attracted by the activities of nature; they are by your side, you feel yourself to be part of them. I actually met people who thought that you even don't have to eat properly there—eating goes of its own accord within that natural world. So the Druid priest would stand in that natural world—but with the whole of his sun initiation—and see what I have described: sun, moon, mediated by the earth's activities, plant growth, growth of root, leaves and flowers, and all of it not in the kind of abstract natural laws we know today but in living elemental spirits. Different elemental spirits are active in the root, different sun elementals, different moon elementals, from those in leaf and flower.

The Druid priest also knew how to find the things that live in beneficent boundaries in root, leaf and flower in the far horizons of nature. Having the gift of imagination he saw the small elemental spirits held in close confinement in the root. He knew that something which was beneficent in the root could emancipate and grow to giant size. He therefore saw the great events in nature as the small natural processes in the plant grown to giant size. As he had spoken of elemental spirits living in the root, so he would speak of the root spirits which had grown further in a way that was cosmically wrong and become visible in the development of hoar frost, dew and hail. He would speak of root spirits working in a beneficent way, and of ice and frost giants which were the same as root spirits grown to giant size in nature. He spoke of the small-scale activities of elementals in the leaf as they fill themselves with the principle that is active in the air. And he would also trace this to the far horizons of nature and speak of the way in which the principle that lives in the plant leaf may become emancipated and seek to go beyond the boundaries of beneficence into the far reaches of nature to embrace the principle that is borne on the waves of the wind. The wind and storm giants are the plant leaf's elementals grown large. The principle in the flower that boils up towards the light of the sun, producing the volatile oils which are phosphoric by nature, when that is emancipated it turns into the fire giants. Loki belonged to that race of giants. With his sun and moon science, the Druid priest would see as one the quality that lived in the confined space of the plant and the emancipated power that lived in wind and weather.

He would go further than that, however. He would say to himself, 'Held within the beneficent boundaries set by the good gods, it unfolds normal plant growth. When it shows itself in frost and ice, it is the product of the gods' enemies. Having grown beyond the set boundaries, the elemental spirits have become enemies of the gods and changed over into the devastating, harmful elements in nature. As a human being I can take in the devastating activities of the gods' enemies. I can therefore gather in the frost and the ice, the powers that ride on the wings of the storm, and all that can be captured on the waves of the wind or in the rain. I can use it for the things I prepare by using the powers of the giants, burning the plant and reducing it to ash, to coal, and so on. I take the powers of the giants and use the powers of the frost, the hail, the raindrops and other such things, and the forces of the fire giants to protect normal plant growth. I rob the giants of all these things so that I may treat the normal plant with it, make medicines from the plants which are kept in their normal boundaries by the beneficent elementals by treating them with the powers of these enemies of the gods.' That was one of the methods of making plants into medicines, using frost, using what lives in snow and ice formations, using what could be achieved by means of combustion, or calcination, and so on. The Druid priest thus felt himself to be the one who took the harmful principles from the enemies of the gods, the giants, and took it back again to serve the good gods. This is how we can follow up these things in many different ways.

Why do we follow these things up? Because we want to be clear in our minds in using this example—I am giving it as an example because I feel that the course given in Penmaenmawr must indeed count as a most important event in the history of the anthroposophical movement—to show that relatively speaking not all that long ago the whole state of the human soul was very different from what it is today. Today people are in a state of mind which absolutely cannot enter into the minds of those earlier peoples. And what I have said about those earlier people could be said about other peoples. We are gaining insight into a completely different state of soul. Those people did not yet have the feeling for the abstract thoughts we have today. All their thinking was still more dreamlike. They did not live in the sharply defined concepts and ideas in which we live today. They were really living in much more lively, rich, saturated dreams, and also in their waking hours as if in a continuation of their dreams. This dreaming, never coming wholly awake, alternated—just as our waking hours today with the abstract ideas of the waking state alternate with dreaming and sleep—with dreamless sleep. Their dreamless sleep was not as we know it today. When the human being came awake for his dreamlike daytime life he would feel, 'Something by way of sleep lives in me even when I am awake. It is something which fills me like inner food for the soul which I have taken in during sleep; it makes itself felt in me, I even have the taste of it within me.' People then still had the aftertaste of sleep in the whole of their organism. A third state was deeper than our sleep today, a state no longer experienced in the human mind. That third state was the state of being embraced by the earth, so that on waking the human being would feel, 'I have not just been sleeping; apart from being asleep, of which I have an aftertaste, I was received by the forces of earth's gravity into a kind of night-time grave. Earth's gravity covered me, I was embraced by the earth.'

We can say that today human beings know three states of consciousness—waking, dreaming, sleeping. And therefore we have to say that at a particular time in the past people knew the states of dreaming, sleeping, being embraced by the earth. Everything that evolves in the course of history is connected to a degree, also at the present time. Because of this, some human souls will have something unusual arise within them in a later life on earth, something like a real memory of earlier times connected with their earlier life on earth. This memory, which begins to shine out in such people, something abnormal in their own time, is like a living memorial in the soul. One such spirit was Jacob Boehme,[58] another Swedenborg.[59] Something connected with the evolution of humanity shines into humanity of more recent times from a far distant past.

Tomorrow I will speak of the inner nature of Jacob Boehme and of Swedenborg, so that we may understand the human past, and the three states of awareness which human beings will have in the future.

LECTURE 7

YESTERDAY my aim was to show the state of mind or soul which people living in a particular region had at an earlier time by considering the evolution of Druid culture which is close to our anthroposophical movement at the present time. Going back through three, four, five thousand years in human evolution—it is different for different regions around the globe—we can always enter into such states of mind which were very different. Being states of mind they do, of course, mean that the whole cultural and social direction and guidance of human life is in accord with the conditions for such a state of mind or soul at a given time.

The evolution to which I am referring relates to the gradual unfolding of conscious awareness. People were very different in earlier times compared to today, and will be different again in future times. Conventional history has little to say about this. Because of this, going beyond a few centuries from the historical present, ordinary history largely proves to be illusionary by nature if one seeks real human understanding. Yesterday I said that essentially we will have to observe three states of conscious awareness—inevitably again with many nuances. Waking, dreaming and sleeping, our present-day levels of consciousness—yes, that truly is the present time, admittedly a present time which continues for centuries and indeed millennia but historically speaking makes up the present. Going back to earlier times in human evolution we do not find the waking state with logical sequences of ideas to which I referred yesterday. The further we go back, to begin with, through human evolution, the more do we not find that kind of logical mind. This really only came up in all severity in the fourteenth and fifteenth centuries, its first beginnings having been in the later years of ancient Greek civilization. We do, however, find a much more lively state of mind in earlier times, filled with images and not ideas, and we find this in the whole of humanity.

The natural forces we know today were quite unknown in that form to the people of those earlier times. At the time of which I spoke yesterday, people would not speak of the laws of meteorology governing winds and weather; as I said, they would speak of something that had image nature, of elemental spirits active in the plant world, of giants, spirits active in the winds, the weather, frost and hail, gales and thunder, and so on. Everything seen in nature was alive then. They did not draw logical conclusions. They looked at all the life, activity, billowing and welling forth of spirits in objects and also in the natural phenomena, the elements. The foundation for inner states of soul was entirely different for those earlier people from what it is today. This state of soul was such that people were really much more contained within themselves than we are today. But this inner containment was again different from anything we know today. It was at the same time a state of mind that moved in dream images yet extended out into cosmic space. They would see images but they did not see them in the way in which we have a thought today and the objects are there outside. No, the giants of which they were sentient—frost giants, storm giants, fire giants—and the spirits of which they were sentient in root, leaf and flower, in all these they felt connected with the plant, with roots, leaves, flowers, with the lightning, with the thunder. They did not feel themselves to be separate from outside nature in their inner life, for they lived in the spirit, in images of spirit, in their souls.

It is not exactly in the very earliest times, of which I wrote in my *Occult Science, an Outline*, but in the times which followed, that spiritual investigation shows how that state of mind evoked a quite

specific inner mood in the important nations of those times. There
certainly was a time when people would still inwardly perceive much
of what truly is essential human nature. In the images I have just
mentioned they saw not merely their current existence but also their
life before they came to earth; they looked into a perspective in time
the way we today look into a perspective in space. This was not
memory but vision. They looked beyond their birth into a spiritual
world from which they had come down into human life on earth. It
was natural for these earlier people to look at this pre-earthly existence and be sentient: 'As a human being I am a spirit, for before I
assumed an earthly body I was in the keeping of spirituality, having
my existence there, living my human destiny not yet in a physical
body but in'—if I may put it like this, in spite of it being paradoxical—'a spiritual bodily nature.'

They would have felt it to be utterly absurd to be asked to believe
in the spirit, just as we would find it absurd to believe in mountains.
For we see the mountains. At that time they would see pre-birth life,
though in an inward way, in soul vision. Then came a time when
people did see this inwardly human aspect in the spirit, seeing it as
the events in pre-birth existence, but nature itself, the nature outside
in their surroundings, was becoming more and more of a kind of
riddle. I would say that pure sensory observation was gradually
moving to the fore in human evolution.

In very early times, the times of ancient Indian civilization, which I
described in my *Occult Science, an Outline*, human beings still saw
absolutely everything in the spirit, including the natural world. A
step forward came when vision in the spirit remained inward, and
nature gradually began—if I may put it like this—to be de-spirited.
People felt inwardly that they were spirit of spirit and they looked
out on the flora in flower, on the cloud propelling the lightning from
itself, on the winds and the weather, on the delicate or marvellously
shaped crystals, on hill and vale, on all those things. A certain mood
then arose which one can trace through long periods of time in
spiritual investigation; it came particularly on what was then civilized humanity, a mood which may be said to have been more or less

as follows: 'We are spirit of spirit. In pre-earthly existence we human beings were connected with spirituality. Now we have been placed in a natural environment. We see the beautiful flowers, the huge mountains, nature mightily active in the winds and the weather. But that is no longer spiritual.' The idea of mere nature around one was progressively coming to the fore.

Now, however, the human being—I am of course speaking of the advanced human being, someone whom we might call 'civilized' in the terms of that time—felt that his living body was created from the substances, the physical matter of this natural world which was without spirit, without gods. If something like this were to come to modern people, the people of today, they would speculate, philosophize and reflect on this. That was not the case, at least initially, with the people of an earlier time. They would not reflect, but be sentient of a tremendous disharmony in their inner experiences: 'I am spirit from spirit land, my true human nature comes from divine heights, but I am clothed in something which has been taken from a natural world that seems to be without spirit; my spiritual existence is interwoven with something which does not show me the spirit. My body is of the same substance as the plants flowering in the fields, of the same substance as the water from the clouds and pouring rain. This substance is, however, devoid of gods.' And it would feel to them like being cast out from the spiritual world, cast out into a world to which they did not really belong.

One might reject this mood, sleep through it, which happens with very many moods in our present civilization. But the people who were awake at that time in the past were sentient of it, and humanity develops in moods, in things we feel and not in ideas and thoughts. Even the development of thoughts in our time is but an episodic development—as we shall see in these very lectures—and someone who merely talks in thoughts is really talking in unreality. The very way in which people talk today is a talking in unreality. People who consider themselves to be most practical, downright bursting with arrogance over their practical nature, are essentially the greatest theoreticians. Today theoreticians are sitting in their offices, and of course also occupying university chairs, and in that case I would say it is a matter of course. But they are also sitting in their offices and move around in the world of trade. Everything is set up theoretically, everything caught up in thoughts. That is one episode. Initially there is no truth to it. It will only come to be true when these people are going to be sentient about this life in thoughts and feel about it the way human beings did in the past when nature seemed to them to be devoid of spirit: 'We are cast out, a race that has been cast out; we are outside of the divine and spiritual heights where we really belong, have been placed in a world where as human beings we do not belong.'

One outcome of this mood is something which then came up as a reflection, a revelation of this mood: the notion of the fall into sin. That idea came from a change in conscious awareness. People said to themselves: 'We have been cast out of the spiritual world; that must be because of original sin.' At a particular period the notion of original sin, of the fall of humanity, lived dimly in human minds. We understand this notion of an original sin, a sin committed before time, a fall before time, if we understand how humanity's conscious awareness changed from past to present and future. What people needed when that mood came over them during that period was not a dull theory. It was above all something which could be put in words in such a way that the words could be balm for souls in need of comfort. We then see something we have often referred to as the guidance given to people in the ancient places of rites and religion, in the mysteries, come up again during a period that is approximately the same as the ancient Persian, the ancient Chaldean civilization in the Near East. We see how this came together with the quality which the priests in the mysteries developed and which made them the greatest comforters of humanity. They became comforters. Comfort shone out from the mysteries. For comfort was needed considering how conscious awareness developed at that time. There had to be a soul quality in the words that came to people's hearts and was like a balm, a comforting balm. It was an age which with regard to creativity in religion and the arts was one of magnificent creative power, though in one respect it was different from what it became later. Many of the details in our art, our religious ideas, do still come from that time. And it is above all ritual symbols, ritual images and acts which still go back to those ancient times.

What did those teachers in the mysteries who had to provide comfort draw on? Well, although general waking consciousness consisted in an awareness in images that were very much alive, as I have described it, there were nevertheless three levels of conscious awareness at that time. Where we have sleeping, dreaming and the waking state today, sleep did then not differ from the waking dream state which was the general waking state, as I mentioned yesterday. Sleep, as it is carried out in the general state of awareness we have today, fully paralyses our conscious awareness. For those earlier people, conscious awareness was very dim during sleep, but something did remain behind when they woke up. The way I put it yesterday was that they had an inner aftertaste of sleep on awakening. Most of them felt a certain sweetness of things lived through that would fill the whole of them, not only on the tongue or palate, like an aftertaste. The sweetness of life in sleep spread also into their life during the day. This sweetness marked a healthy state of life to them; when other tastes got mixed in, this would be a sign of sickness. It sounds paradoxical when we say today that in earlier times human beings sensed the sweet after-effect of sleep in their limbs, in their arms and down to the fingertips, in the other parts of their organism. But that is how it was. Spiritual science reveals it. Our language still bears witness to it, though it has become materialistic and less subtle. A sleeping draught was something spiritual in the past; it was sleep itself. It only became something material later on, a fluid which one would be drinking. Sleep itself was a draught from nature, a draught that made the ordinary day-time memory fade away. It was at the same time a draught to make you forget.

Ordinary people had a vague after-sensation, but initiation gave the teachers in the mysteries, leaders of the people, a more accurate awareness of what human beings actually lived through in their sleep. Today, modern initiation takes us from developing ordinary ideas to spirit vision. The people of those earlier times would step down, as it were, from dreamlike waking into the sleep state, but they acquired conscious awareness for it, so that an ordinary person would have the aftertaste, and the mystery priest would in a conscious way feel his way into, grow sentient of, sleep itself and as it were got to know the principle that would then produce the aftertaste, as I have described it. He got to know the waters beyond physical existence, the waters into which the human soul entered in sleep, the waters into which the soul entered, the waters it is immersed in every night. These were the waters of the nature and activity of the astral world. Compared to waking dreams this, however, was merely the second state or condition.

The third state was one of which present-day humanity does not know anything at all, a state deeper than the dreamless sleep of today. Yesterday I said we should call it being embraced by the earth. Every human being was in that state in the middle of the night's deep sleep. But only the mystery priest, being initiated, was able to have conscious awareness of what one found there, was able to convey the results of this conscious awareness, and that was the science of that day. People would then not merely say, 'I am embraced by the earth.' Yes, they would say that as well, but they also said something else. Yes, they would say to themselves, 'I am embraced by the earth,' but be sentient of something as if in the everyday course of life they had entered into a state that was really already very close to death, but a death from which one would awaken again. In this state of conscious awareness they would feel as if they had really gone down into the earth, as if they had already been put into a grave, though this would not be an earthly grave. This grave was not merely produced as an idea but had to be produced as an idea, and I can illustrate this for you in the following way.

You see, the sun's rays do not merely come down to earth and give lustre to the flowers, shine out from the stars. A farmer is more aware of this than a city person, for he also makes use of the way the sun's heat entered into the earth in winter. The heat which has streamed into the earth in the summer is there in the soil then. And not only the heat, other powers of the sun also stream into the earth. But from the point of view from which I am now speaking this was actually less important. The more important thing was that the moon influences could also penetrate the earth, going down below the surface of the earth, as it were. I would say that it was a beautiful idea in those old days, not just poetic but hyper-poetic, that people had an image, not just a logical view but an image of how silvery sunlight streamed down in the light of the full moon and then entered right into the earth, an image of this moon silver penetrating a certain distance into the soil and then shining back again, from the inner earth, having been taken in by the earth, and not from the surface. People felt that the way the silvery moon billowed and welled, shining in and shining out, flowing in and out in billows—this was not just a beautiful image. As a mystery priest one would know something quite specific about this billowing, welling moonlight.

They knew that human beings are subject to gravity on earth. Gravity, gravitation, keeps them grounded, and in a way the earth keeps its creatures close to it with gravity. The priest knew that the moon powers counteracted gravity. It is just that they are generally weaker than the more robust gravity of earth, but it is they which counteract the forces of gravity on earth. They knew this. They knew that human beings were not just a lump held fast by earth's gravity, but that they were in a kind of equilibrium, attracted by the earth, drawn away by the moon, though earth's gravity had the upper hand for human beings on earth. However, this negative gravity—I'd say, this gravity which drew away—did take effect for the element that was active in the human head. Although it did not enable one to fly, one could elevate one's spirit to the starry heavens. With this initiation, by the roundabout route via the moon's influences, the mystery priests of that time helped people to know the influences that the surrounding stars have on human beings on earth.

That was the astrological initiation which is so much misused today. It was particularly marked among the Chaldaeans. In this roundabout way they knew something not only about the moon's influences, but also about the influences of the sun, of Mars, Saturn and so on. Today man has become—forgive me for presenting this, too, in the form of an image, but such things are difficult to characterize logically—man is an earthworm today where knowledge is concerned, no, not even an earthworm, something worse. Man has turned into an earthworm for which there is never any rain, which never emerges from the soil. Earthworms emerge from the soil at certain times, when it is raining, and they then have a part in what goes on above ground, which is of benefit to them. Today man is an earthworm in soul and spirit for which there is never any rain. He is completely encapsulated where the earthly sphere is concerned. He'll think, for instance, 'The parts of my body simply grow in about the same way as stones also develop on earth.' Modern people do not know, of course, that their hair, the hairs on their head, results from sun influences, and so forth, for they are earthworms for which there is never any rain, bearing the sun influences within them but never coming up to the surface to investigate anything of this kind. The priests at the ancient mysteries knew very well that man has not grown from the soil like a head of cabbage but has come into being thanks to the concerted efforts of the whole starry cosmos around him. So you see how in the past people related to their initiated guides in the mysteries who had been initiated in the way I have shown and knew what the cosmic surroundings of the earth had to signify for human beings.

This made it possible for the priests to tell something to people which I am going to put in fairly commonplace words, for today we are not as yet in a position to speak in the way of those priests in the ancient mysteries who would also put things in marvellous poetic form. This was possible with the genius of language at that time. Today we cannot speak like that for our language does not make it possible. Today we might put the things the priests in the mysteries said to the people who looked to them for comfort in a natural world without spirit into which they felt they had been banished in the following words: 'Yes, for as long as you are in life in the states of ordinary waking consciousness, your environment will seem to you to be without spirit.' However, if we enter consciously into the regions around the world where we see the gods of the stars active in the light of the silvery moon which flows and billows through the earth—if we can do that we learn to see—no longer of its own accord, which was the case in earlier times, but through human effort—that spirits are after all present everywhere in this outside natural world, a nature which bears within it gifts of the gods, spirits, elemental spirits. And so the comfort which the priests in the mysteries would give to people in those ancient times was that they made them aware that plants are not just beautiful, they are truly also filled with spiritual activity and spiritual beings, that the clouds do not just move majestically through the air but that divine elemental spirits are active in them, and so on. As initiates, the priests guided those whom they had to guide to the spirit in nature.

At a particular stage of human evolution it was the function of the mysteries to tell people, 'It is merely an illusion, part of waking dream life, that nature is without spirit. In reality spirit may be found everywhere in the natural world.'

So there was once a human past when human beings actually lived within the spirituality of existence in this way and, thanks to the institution of the mysteries, learned of the spirituality of existence also in the sphere that initially seemed to them to be devoid of spirit. Everything which thus came to human beings, be it from instinct, for instance vision of the inner spirituality, or from being taught in the mysteries, for instance that the spirit is all-present in nature, did after all make them dependent, dependent on spirituality. If things had continued like this in human evolution, something which today we have to admit is one of the greatest privileges, perhaps even the central privilege for humanity, could never have come to conscious awareness, and that is sentience of free will, the sense of freedom.

The state of mind where spirituality was sensed instinctively had to fade away. Humanity had to be taken to other states of mind. That sense of being embraced by the earth, which gave the ancient initiates the power to draw on star wisdom and hence the spirituality of nature, fell into complete decay. Only dreamless sleep, dreaming and the waking state remained for the human soul. We might say that the region of mind in which freedom would be able to dawn was added at the other end. The wide-awake state of mind in which we have our everyday life and pursuit of knowledge today was something totally unknown to an earlier humanity. But this was where the possibility arose for pure thought, the existence of which may make us despair,[60] but from which alone we can gain the impulses for freedom. If humanity had never gained this faculty of pure thought, which does not at the same time establish existence but is pure thought, neither would we ever have gained awareness of freedom.

I'd like to say that the connection of man with spirituality which had existed lay in darkness behind human evolution. Instead, human beings gained these three states of conscious awareness, and these actually took them from spiritual heights down into depths of earth. But they were meant to find their very own power to develop freedom from those very depths. Essentially, the dawn of this state of soul—waking, dreaming and sleeping—had already been there for a thousand years. Humanity had moved a long way into a particular darkness, the darkness in which the impulse for freedom lies but the light of spirituality does not shine. Do develop a real feeling for the way this really was in human evolution. Looking back into an early age, we see human beings looking up into the starry heavens, and out of the knowledge they had of those starry heavens, saying to themselves: 'The powers of those starry heavens live in me; I am part of this cosmos.' As a spirit, man had been forced down to earth. The heavens had grown dark, so to say, for human beings were not able to see through, to understand the light, even sunlight or the light of the stars, all that shone down in a physical way. It was as if a curtain had come down, and human beings could not find support in any way for their existence. They could no longer see anything that was behind the curtain.

Tomorrow we shall see that this curtain had actually been there for a thousand years, how it grew denser and denser, and how this density of the curtain was reflected in the whole mood of humanity. Then a light came through the curtain, and the curtain fell apart, as it were. This was the light that arose on Golgotha. The event on Golgotha entered into human evolution. In this event, an event that happened on earth, human beings were to see again what they had once seen in the vastness of the cosmos as the spirituality of the world. In going through the Mystery on Golgotha the Christ was to bring something which in earlier times had been seen in the heavens into life on earth. The divine spirit, the Christ, was to descend and dwell in a human body, to bring this light in a new and different way to a humanity which was then unable to come away from the earth.

As human beings we are today only beginning to understand this Mystery on Golgotha, and the future of earth evolution will have to consist in this Mystery on Golgotha being understood by humanity with ever greater maturity, and that the glory coming from the Mystery on Golgotha would be understood more and more, with inner glory becoming cosmic glory and beginning to shine out over everything that human beings are able to look into. Before we can consider this we need to add some further building blocks today.

In a certain respect, things that have once been alive in humanity's evolution on earth will also come back again. As I have told you, the priests in the mysteries were alive to this way of looking into the moon influences. Those moon influences took them up into their astrological initiation. They learned how it was possible to be initiated into the star secrets of the cosmos through the moon influences. An important aspect of this initiation was that something would come over the individual who was to be initiated, as if he suddenly felt within himself that gravity, weight, had less significance for him than usually. He was less aware of his weight. His teachers, who were older, told him not to give in to this, but to make a great effort of will when he felt himself to grow lighter, as it were, and give himself weight. That was, in a way, part of the craft learned in the old initiations, that one let natural weight which had been lost under the influence of the moon flow back into oneself again by effort of will. And with that the star wisdom would shine out. That is how all the potential a human being had at that time to overcome gravity was used to develop the will in him to hold fast to the earth in his soul. Holding on to the earth in one's soul was like lighting an inner light in the soul, to shine out into the vast cosmos. Man then became familiar with that vast cosmos.

When spiritual science casts a light on these things, one can give an exact description of how this ancient state of mind arose. But this principle, which existed in those human beings, does also recur. There is such a thing as atavism, with ancient faculties being transmitted. It comes back again, for human beings do after all also come back again. When the connection with the powers of the moon comes up again in people who live in a later age where it really should no longer exist, since that deep sleep no longer exists, it becomes somnambulism, especially the ordinary kind of lunatism or sleep-walking. These people do not fight the getting lighter but walk about on roofs or at least leave their beds. They are doing something with their essential human nature which really only the astral body should do. Something which at such a later time may be said to be abnormal had in earlier times been a special asset which could be used to gain insight. The popular term 'moon sick' for such people made good sense, for this condition is connected with an atavistic relationship with the moon powers which has persisted from ancient times.

Human beings are thus related to the powers of the moon, as I have described. They are just as much related to the powers of the sun. It is merely that this relationship with the powers of the sun is active in a hidden way, and one only comes to it in a most indirect way. Undoubtedly it was the Druid priests of the flowering and not the period of decay who looked for their sun initiation in that relationship with the powers of the sun. That sun initiation led to a condition where one was looking up, not only stimulated, in a way, by the powers of the moon to gain some knowledge of the secrets of the cosmos in the astrological initiation. No, this sun initiation did already provide some kind of dialogue with the divine spirits in the universe, a kind of inspiration, whereas the moon initiation provided only a kind of vision in images. Sun initiation meant that one would in a way hear the advice of the spirits. Above all one's eyes are now made to receive the physical rays of the sun. I mentioned yesterday that qualities of spirit and soul are present in these physical sun-rays. It is just that modern people do not see this. Their attitude to the sun is like the attitude of one person meeting another, with that other individual claiming to have an inner soul, and the first individual saying to the second: 'No such thing as soul. When you move an arm, it is a matter of leverage, with strings, your muscles; when they are contracted the lever is drawn up. It is a mechanism.' That is the modern-day attitude to the influence of the sun. People see only the external and physical, in this case merely physical light. Yet the spirituality of sun nature enters into us at the same time as the physical light does. With a particular kind of inner concentration, not the one I described in my *Knowledge of the Higher Worlds* but one that is like an elemental force due to atavism, human beings can today—with 'today' I mean the historic period of time which may, of course, continue for centuries—cease to be highly receptive to the physical influence of the sun and instead grow receptive to spiritual sun nature. They then see things in a different way. Where this atavistic element appears one sees things differently from the way one does in ordinary life today. When you look in a mirror, the mirror reflects what is in front of it. When someone has the constitution of soul where in spite of being fully sensible he does not look into the sun, does not see the physical light of the sun but sees absolute darkness, then this darkness becomes a mirror and reflects his immediate surroundings, the natural world. He will then not say, 'This is a plant; it has a root; it produces leaves, its flower, fruit and seed.' He will say, 'In the lower part of the plant I see elemental spirituality of wisdom and this has a quality of preservation, of consolidation. Further up the plant I see this quality of preservation, of consolidation being overcome, with the plant seeking not to consolidate but to alternate between consolidation and dissolution in leaf development, and finally I see the plant strive upwards and it is like a cooking process due to the action of fire.' The life of the plant is then mirrored in the darkness, which spiritually, however, is light—similar to the way in which Jacob Boehme[61] saw the plant atavistically, seeing salt nature below, mercurial nature in the middle, and phosphorus nature up above. We see the quality which in early times was part of human civilization, original civilization when one was not yet able to read and write, influencing a mind such as that of Jacob Boehme who was a natural sun initiate. If one is not able to read a work such as his *Mysterium magnum*, *De signatura rerum*, *Aurora the Day-Spring* and so forth in such a way, as it were, that his halting words tell one something very similar to the things I have been telling you about the Druid priests, then one is reading Jacob Boehme the wrong way. He had not been initiated in an outward way, but something like the recapitulation of an earlier existence on earth welled up in his inmost being, and that was this sun initiation. You can trace this even in his biography.

Even more profound powers that may influence human beings come from what initially was the outermost planet in our planetary system. It is not the outermost one in modern astronomy, for two more have been added, which are some matter of concern even in modern physical astronomy because the laws governing the movements of their moons are not quite right, and so on. They are included, however, because position in space is considered most important, and since Uranus and Neptune have joined as well, people do include them. But as I said, they are something of a pain because their moons have 'gone off course' relative to what the other, 'decent' moons of Jupiter and so on are doing. In real terms we may after all say that for a living, concrete understanding of the planetary system Saturn definitely is the outermost planet. Human beings can be under the influence of the moon, which I have described in more detail, or the influence of the sun, which I outlined briefly. They can also be under the influence of these Saturn actions. In its spiritual emanation into the planetary system and hence into human beings, Saturn is a kind of cosmic historic memory. It is like the memory, the remembering process, in our planetary system, and if we want to know anything about what is going on in the planetary system, astronomical speculation certainly will not tell us.

Today these things are beginning to make people working in external science desperate, for nothing is really quite right. But they are setting about it all in the wrong way. You see, among ourselves we, too, have often spoken of the theory of relativity, as it is called, saying that one can never really speak of absolute movement in the physical world, but must always refer to relative movement. Just as one may say, 'The sun is moving, the earth is standing still,' so did people later come to say, 'The earth is moving and the sun is standing still.' All of it is merely relative and one can say the one thing or the other. At a conference of the anthroposophical movement held here in Stuttgart, people were one day speaking of the theory of relativity. A follower of this theory showed the audience in a very simple way that it does not matter if you take a match and move it along a matchbox which you are holding, or if you hold the match still and move the box. This will also ignite it. This was a serious scientific subject presented in all seriousness, and one cannot really say anything against it. There might have been a naive individual who might have nailed the matchbox to something, and then there would have been something absolute in it. Or perhaps one could have pushed back the whole house (Landhausstrasse 70 it was at the time), that would have restored relativity, though it would have been a bit difficult. But if we extend it to the whole physical universe we could agree with Einstein and say: 'Nothing absolute is to be found in the physical world; everything is definitely relative there.' But people stop at relativity. It is exactly the relativity of the physical world which must make us realize that the absolute must not be sought in the physical but in the spiritual world. Science is everywhere providing access to the spiritual world, but it has to be rightly understood. No need today to be an amateur. You can be an exact, genuine scientist, and true science will take you to the spirit. It is just that it is not thought all the way through, not even by its leading experts. Because of it, nothing can also be said in physical studies about something like the Saturn of our universe. Saturn is the remembrance, the memory for our planetary system, as it were. Everything that has happened in the planetary system is archived in it.

The connection with the moon may come up one-sidedly in a person, like something inherited from earlier human evolution, something passed down from past humanity, and the person then becomes a sleepwalker, and the spiritual influences of the sun may come up again and the individual is then actually looking into absolute darkness with open eyes and not in the usual way into the light, a darkness in which nature is mirrored, so that the individual sees things as Jacob Boehme did. In the same way one can also enter into relationship with the Saturn influences, which affects mainly the human head, actually implanting the passing memory during earthly life in the human being. These Saturn influences are particularly likely to show themselves.

We may thus speak of moon people, the ordinary sleepwalkers, and of sun people such as Jacob Boehme, even Paracelsus,[62] though to a lesser degree. We may also speak of Saturn people. Swedenborg was a Saturn individual. He was another one who we can't say makes but who should make the usual kind of scholars rack their brains. For in ordinary science Swedenborg truly was an authority at the height of his time. Until he reached his forties he was also reasonably acceptable in this science of ours, saying nothing but things that external science was able to go along with. Then, however, Swedenborg was gradually befogged. We have to say that Saturn powers grew particularly active in him. People who base themselves on materialism say that he went mad. But it should really be something to make us think that so many works by him, post-humously published by a Swedish Society, are considered to be scientific. Important Swedish scholars are now involved in publishing them. These are however the works that he wrote *before* he had his spiritual vision—as we'll call it for now. It is difficult to speak of someone who was, as it were, the most intelligent individual in his time until he came into his forties, and with regard to whom one really has to say in his later years, 'He's a fool, to put it mildly.' Swedenborg absolutely did not grow more stupid but there was a particular moment, just when he had risen to the pinnacle of the ordinary science of his time, when he began to see into the spiritual world. As this took hold of his head, the organ, as it were, which he truly had developed quite specifically, he was able to look in his own way—not the way in which Jacob Boehme saw the inner secrets of nature mirrored in the darkness—into the immediate ether, there where the images of higher spirituality appear in the ether. He described this spiritual world very much in his own way. His vision was not as he had imagined. The spirits to which he refers are different. Yet he did not just see these spirits mirrored by the earth, but he saw their influences in the ether, he saw ether configurations. Those were the acts of the spirits—which did not become visible themselves—in the earth's ether. Jacob Boehme saw nature mirrored, Swedenborg saw what the spirits brought about in the ether, spirits of which he saw only the influences they had. So when Swedenborg describes angels, these are not angels but configurations in the ether. These were, however, brought about by angels, a reflection of what the angel does. It is always important to consider the reality of such things. It is wrong, of course, to say that Swedenborg saw the spiritual world as such, for he did not have that power. But he did see something that was real.

The ordinary sleepwalker, the moon-sick individual, does something real. He does with his physical body what he should only be doing with his astral body. Jacob Boehme first saw in such a way with his physical body, above all with the arrangement of his eyes, that he excluded the physical, looking into darkness, but saw the light in the darkness, mirroring the nature spirits. Swedenborg did not see mirror images but the ether images of a higher spiritual existence. So there are stages from the unseeing, automatic state of being filled with the spirit of the sleepwalker to what I'd call the natural second sight of Jacob Boehme, who did not see the outer aspect of nature but the reflection of the inner aspect, and all the way up to Swedenborg who saw not mirror images but reality in the ether, the images—not mirror images—of the activities or proceedings up above, in the higher spiritual regions.

We see, therefore, that we may speak of a human past and present, with the past still to be found in the present, with definite signs, like a legacy, taking the form of abnormal states which need to be understood. If we are thus able to look at the past and at the things which still project from the past into the present, then with the help of a thorough understanding of the Mystery on Golgotha we can also refer to a feeling for what the future will be. This will be in tomorrow's lecture.

LECTURE 8

YOU will have seen from what was said yesterday that a particular state of conscious awareness, one which was still living experience to people in earlier times, has been lost in a way. I did say that the particular kind of waking conscious we have today, living preferably in more or less abstract ideas or at least in shadowy images, did not exist in the same form in the past, but instead there was a kind of waking dream state, dreamy waking state. One could not be sentient of it the way we are of a dream today, but it was like the epitome of living images which corresponded to a more or less spiritual reality. A kind of sleep state existed then which was dreamless, but left the kind of aftertaste I have described for you. Then there was also a third state of mind, the one which afterwards was really felt to be like resting in the welling moon powers which enter into the earth and really do in a way raise human beings above earthly gravity, letting them be sentient of cosmic existence. The essential thing with the old states of mind was that people were also sentient of man's cosmic existence. Today, in our ordinary state of conscious awareness, only a shadowy afterglow remains, an afterglow of which only very few people are aware. It simply passes by the human mind without our being aware of it.

Let me characterize this state of mind in most ancient times. When people consider their dreams today they will find that all kinds of things they have lived through here on earth flow into these dreams, which in a way are chaotic. Long forgotten things come up, changed in many different ways; even things that went unnoticed in life may come up in one's dreams. The times when these things happened are also mixed up in all kinds of ways. But when one goes into these dream experiences in more detail one will discover something most peculiar. One will find that essentially everything that comes up as part of the dream is in some way, however tenuously, connected with events in the last three days. You may dream that something has come up again which you may have lived through 25 years ago. It is there, full of life, with perhaps some slight changes, but it is there. Yet if you look at it a bit more closely you will always discover something like the following. Someone comes into this dream which brings back an event that was 25 years ago; to be really abstract, let us say this person is called Edward. You will at least find that somewhere you heard the word Edward, even if only a whisper passing your ear, or have read it, quietly moving past your eye. Any event, however insignificant or remote, that comes up in a dream will be connected with something or other from the last three days. This is because human beings really bear experiences of two, three or four days ago—such times can only be approximate—in them in a wholly different way from the way they do anything that happened earlier than that.

Human beings initially take their perceptions up into their astral organism and their I organism. The events perceived will at first live a life that is directly connected with their conscious awareness. Anything experienced in the course of three days touches our feelings in a much more intense way than do events that lie more than three days back. As I said, in ordinary life we do not pay attention to these things, but they are something real after all. The reason is that anything by way of perceptions or thought processes taken into the human astral organism and into the I organism has to be impressed into the ether body or body of creative powers, and also at least in some respect into the physical body. The making of this impression takes two, three, four days, so that we have taken something we have experienced two and three times through the night before it has been impressed in the ether body and in the physical body. Only then may it be said to have become so fixed, at least in the ether body, that it can now be permanently remembered thought for us. There really is a continuous inner interaction in human beings, a kind of struggle between the astral body and the ether body, and the outcome of the struggle is always that something which the individual had initially experienced as a spirit endowed with conscious awareness imprints, configures itself into the denser, more material elements of his essential nature. After three or four days we then take something which before had been just a passing sensory experience with us as an entry made, as it were, in our ether or creative powers body and in our physical body.

Do consider, as I give this description, how little of this people are actually aware of at the present time. Yet it is something that goes on all the time in the life of the human mind and also of the body. Every experience we perceive must essentially wait for three or four days before it is wholly ours. It swings to and fro between astral body and ether body, and in a way does not really know if it will indeed be imprinted in the ether body and with this also in the physical body.

For something happens there that is really extraordinarily important. Just consider that only the I and the astral body are our true self. We cannot say that the ether body is ours. People of this materialistic age are presumptive enough to declare their ether body and above all their physical body to be *their* body. But those bodies actually belong wholly to the cosmos. When something we experience in the I and astral body is handed over to the ether body and physical body in three or four days' time it is no longer ours alone but belongs to the cosmos. It is really only for three days that we can say that something we have dealt with in the world has significance only for us. In three or four days' time we have inscribed it in the universe; it rests in the universe, belonging not only to us but also to the gods.

In very early times of human evolution the state of conscious awareness that was deeper than sleep and has now been lost gave people distinct sentience of this strange fact. And the initiates were able to say what was really behind this strange sentience. Above all in the period of which I spoke yesterday, that of Egypto-Chaldean civilization, it was merely a dim feeling that people had. But the initiates of the mysteries were initiated into the actual nature of it and this happened because at that time—today initiation has to be an entirely inward process in soul and spirit, at most involving also bodily symbols and body image processes—initiation was essentially an external process, with the external changes then also changing the inner aspects. In many cases initiation was such—I am giving one example but could also give others—that the initiand was for about three days taken by his initiators into a state that has really been lost today. He was in that state for three days to live through the things that a human being goes through in the world outside the human being for those three days, and how this passed over, as it were, into the actual nature of the human being. The initiated individual arrived at the view as to what an idea, sentience, a feeling for facts goes through before a person can make it his own. But what came up there was in a state that was so much hidden within this wisdom, and does contain elements of extraordinary significance—so significant that modern materialists have not the least idea of it. It is the following.

It will be easiest for me to help you to understand what was achieved with this initiation where the initiand was kept in a state of dim consciousness for three days if I first remind you of the life in dreams that everyone still knows today. Yes, the life in dreams is something that needs to be studied in detail. We must of course avoid all the superstition, and this must be understood if one goes deeply into dream life taking a pure view, the view where one is seeking to gain genuine knowledge, but it is something which has extraordinary depth.

How does this dream life actually show itself? Well, we know many different kinds of dreams, but let us concentrate on the kind of dream that is a reminiscence of past events. The images of those events come up in these dreams. How do they present? Well, you know that they have been transformed to a great, an extraordinarily great degree. It can certainly be the case that someone who perhaps has not the least prospect of ever doing such a thing in his real life dreams that as a tailor he has to make a ceremonial coat for a high-ranking minister. He may not have the least prospect of doing so, but he is always making and has always made coats, perhaps even coats he was pleased with. Well, all kinds of things may play into such a dream. Perhaps the individual concerned was the servant of a Roman senator in a previous life on earth and had to dress the senator in his toga. Dim powers of sentience remain, and something he is going through in this life is tinged with something that shines across from earlier lives on earth.

I have referred to only one of the causes for dreams changing in content. But still, they do change greatly, which is something we all know. And one really has to ask oneself, 'What do these dreams contain? What is active in them?' It is after all external events which trigger such dreams, but these external events have been completely transformed in the dream.

Why is that so? You see, it comes from something which the natural-scientific view would never let us dream of the least little bit today. This is because the laws accepted in natural science today are looked for everywhere in the outside world by observation and experimentation. These natural laws to which I am referring come to a halt as soon as they reach the human skin. If someone believes that the natural laws he establishes in his laboratory also act within boundaries set by the human skin he is definitely on the wrong track. It is not only that the substances taken into his organism are changed within it. The active movement of the organic laws to which the human being is subject live in the dream. The dream is closer to us than the abstract thinking we do during the day. The dream contains the manner in which the external substances behave inside the human being, taking the form of laws. And how does the dream present? As a protest against the reality framed as the laws of nature. From going to sleep until you wake up you live in the world of which scientists say that everything in the world goes according to these laws. The moment when you pierce through your dream into the spiritual world just the tiniest bit, a small spider's web, I'd say, your dream experience shows itself to be a protest against the laws of nature. The dream cannot proceed the way events proceeded in the outside world, otherwise you would be very close to waking up. The dream that arises from actual sleep is a protest, the way it hangs together, against the laws of nature. For it comes closer to the human being.

Present-day materialistically minded people make interesting discoveries in this respect. An interesting book, published years ago, can really only be said to be truly characteristic of the mental constitution particularly of modern people who think in a scientific way. It is *Die Magie als experimentelle Naturwissenschaft* [magic as experimental natural science] by a man called Staudenmaier.[63] Some of you will know the book. The man also wanted to find out if there really is anything to the spiritual world. As to anthroposophy, he confessed that he had only read the writings of its opponents. People are hesitant to set about it, because they find it difficult to get a grip on anthroposophy. It is particularly if they are part of the scientific structure of today that they do not easily find their way into anthroposophy. He started by making experiments to find out about the world of the spirits, rather like spiritualism. He reduced his conscious awareness, made himself fuddled, until he entered into a medium-like state. He then did automatic writing. But he was surprised to find that it was a lot of nonsense, and none of it agreed with what he otherwise knew to be real. It would not fit. Above all it was odd that the automatic writing said that spirits spoke to him. For he knew very well that it was not possible for spirits to speak to him. Moreover those non-spirits told the most terrible lies. Indeed, he grew quite—I don't want to speak badly of him—well, medial, completely losing his way in the whole business. A friend suggested that he let it be and live a sensible life, go hunting, for instance. So he went hunting, hunting for magpies. Lo and behold, the things he had stirred up in himself continued even into his hunting. He could not get rid of them. When he looked up into a tree he would see not a magpie but a frightful dragon with terrible claws which looked at him with fearsome eyes, absolutely horrible! And such stuff was everywhere. He then lived in a continuous inner battle, seeking to find his way back to being a normal human being.

I am telling you this because this is experimental evidence that everywhere, the moment one is not merely in a waking dream but uses machinations that take one to the situation where the inner human being also has its say, you do immediately get the protest against the external natural order. Which is of course felt to be a lie. If you are used to seeing someone who is your friend always as a reasonably decent individual and then, when you are in this state, you find that he is all the time sticking out his tongue at you, thumbing his nose at you and grinning at you, you'll say, 'The spiritual world is telling lies.' One is really acting like the dream in such a case. Now, the correct element in this is that in every case where a human being comes to the spiritual world of which he is part with everything that is inside his skin he enters into an existence that will protest against the natural order. No wonder that all kinds of elemental spirits turn up in all those falsehoods when the case is undeveloped and one cannot judge the situation. But you always get protest against the natural order when you come to the spiritual, as even ordinary dreams do show.

People should really say to themselves, 'I am entering into a very different order there, and though it only comes in the fleeting form of a dream it does come as a protest against the best of natural laws which one can outwardly establish in laboratory and experiment.' But you see, this is the first step towards the spiritual world. At this first stage one meets the protest against the laws of nature. The laws of nature lose their majesty, I would say, as soon as one enters into the inner nature of man.

Going through those three days the old initiates came to understand that there is not just a natural order but within and behind it there is a spiritual order. Someone who gets acquainted with initiation in this way can enter into these things even today, using present-day means, can go through the experiences of the three days when coming to experience for the first time what is really a dreadful torment for the soul. For there the human being is indeed entering into a world where all natural laws collapse, where dreams are ever-changing, where situations keep changing even where reminiscences of ordinary life are concerned, for the laws of nature do no longer apply. If the laws of nature are everything to you, you will to begin with face nothingness, the void.

It is particularly painful, deeply painful and tragic for modern human beings to go through this initiation and be sentient of entering a region of existence where this protest against the laws of nature is uttered. One feels that everything one has had before in the intellect, which was, of course, based on the laws of nature, this intellectualistic soul quality is drowning. One's soul can no longer breathe because one has got too much used to the natural order. Finally one sees that a different world is coming in from a completely different side of the world. This lives not in a natural but in a spiritual order. And from the depths of human conscience one is sentient of a moral world order which is present throughout in and welling through that natural world order. One learns to say to oneself: 'Here is the natural order; my senses perceive it, and natural science establishes its laws. When I leave this natural order I enter into a world that protests against it. As I become aware of this protest against the natural order, the moral world order pours in all around like a new, light-filled water of life, so that one may breathe again. This moral world order ultimately opens out and becomes spiritual world order.' That was the great insight that the initiates of earlier times had. They saw the real moral world order project into the physically real world order. In between they experienced the protest against the physical world order. A faint last glimmer of this is experienced in the three-day event of which I spoke. Anything we live through in the outside world, be it our sensations, be it our actions, needs three or four days to be imprinted in our organism. But when it has been imprinted it is not in the form in which we experienced it outwardly; it is imprinted as an impulse that calls for a moral development, which is entirely different in its laws from the natural order. If someone were to see what has become of his experiences within him after those three days, he would say to himself: 'Something I lived through in a natural way in earthly existence has become imprinted in the eternal core of my being. It is no less real than it was in the outside world, but now lives in me as the impulse of a moral world order, following which I now go further out on the ocean of life.' In this way we bear within us the moral causes for our later life and these have evolved from the events we experienced in the natural world.

However, in the last periods of human evolution the situation was that as the human being entered into that sub-sleep, as I'd call it, into the state of being embraced by the earth, he was entering into the external ether. There the things he had experienced were balanced out with the external ether. Morally human beings were placed into the moral world order not only with regard to their inner orientation but they were placed in the morality of the cosmos in that sub-sleep, being embraced by the earth. This was lost to humanity when this deep sleep was eliminated from human states of conscious awareness, so that only that faint echo remained in the three-day experience which I described for you. Humanity would have been gradually cast out from the self-understood moral world order, as it were, if there had not been another event in the course of earth evolution. It was an event in world history, when the Christ spirit went through the process that individual initiates had gone through in earlier times so that they might tell people what had been experienced in the three days. The Christ spirit, having descended from spiritual worlds into the body of Jesus of Nazareth and as a god living an actual human life, went through this in a unique event on earth. He went through the process that had been gone through in those three days, doing so for the whole of humanity. The knowledge that before could be gained through the very deep sleep (coming to man not consciously but at least subconsciously), something human beings had gone through in a wholly nature-related way, had to be gone through so that human beings might be able to connect with the deed that the Christ did for earthly humanity in the Mystery on Golgotha. That was the deed a god did on our behalf. Man had taken a sudden step in the evolution of the conscious mind, and because of this he had to live in a moral way and with regard to Christ Jesus, through something that he had earlier experienced by nature. The coming of the Mystery on Golgotha thus relates to the whole meaning of earth evolution because it did so with the meaning of the evolution of the human mind. We can only understand what was really meant to happen with the Mystery on Golgotha if we look back on something that had once happened naturally and now has to happen in a moral sense.

However, the modern mind, moving between waking, sleeping and dreaming, has not yet gained its inner harmony in this particular respect. For what has been going through this modern mind since it developed its own form, more and more so as time went on, especially from the fifteenth century onwards? A one-sided way of looking at the natural order. Yes, that is what people believe in, and they also think they understand this natural order. They call everything within this natural order real existence. But they do not want to go any further. They do not want to penetrate to that power of human insight which leads to the spiritual. Because of this it came to be accepted in more recent times to speak of the moral world order as of something which now does also come in from somewhere or other. People forgot honesty, however. For when you actually look at the natural order the way people got used to doing more and more, one could not really say that it had any reality. All one could do, I'd say, was to help oneself through the situation in a somewhat dishonest way by saying, 'On the one hand there is knowledge, and on the other hand there is belief. Knowledge cannot be belief, and belief cannot be knowledge, and the moral world order relates to belief.' That is a convenient formula which has been commonly accepted by many in recent times. This distinction between belief and knowledge is actually considered to be truly Christian. It was not all that long ago, relatively speaking, five or six centuries ago, that the distinction certainly was not made in this way, quite definitely not by the earlier Christians. Today it still is not Catholic dogma, but Catholic usage, to distinguish between belief and knowledge in this way. People just do not know how to relate to natural order and moral and spiritual order, because they do not know the transition, they do not understand even how a dream takes one out of the natural order in a protest against it, a dream which in a sense is the great preparer. When we have gone through this preparation we may come upon the principle which is moral world order because it is spiritual moral world order.

A satisfying view on these things can really only be gained if we take an unbiased look into the human past and into something that does not yet exist in the present. Otherwise even the historical documents from the most ancient times will basically continue to be something you stare at but certainly do not understand. You see, this morning people talked in many ways about the people who oppose anthroposophy. There are things we can say in favour of these opponents, but not for the good. With the things the opponents are saying about anthroposophy one—well, at least I—must sometimes recall an anecdote which is said to be based on the truth. Kuno Fischer, the well-known professor,[64] liked to tell it on many occasions. He said that he had two colleagues at school who lived together, may have been brothers. They had an uncle who was an out-and-out simpleton. The time came when they were learning about logarithms in mathematics and needed to buy logarithm tables. The uncle took a look at these tables. He saw nothing but figures on them, and so he asked these schoolboys, his nephews, what kind of figures these were. They had no idea how to introduce him to logarithms. Finally one of the two young rogues had an idea: 'Yes, those are all the house numbers in Europe.' The uncle believed him, and decided that this was really quite useful, to know all the house numbers in London, Paris and so on instantly. You see, just as this uncle regarded the logarithm tables, so do people look at these ancient documents without any inner vision as to what they tell. The scholars who are currently publishing them ultimately also have nothing else to say about them but what the uncle did about the logarithms, thinking them to be house numbers throughout Europe. One merely has to know how far the way of seeing this, which is possible with abstract thought, is removed from the spiritual reality.

This is something one must be really clear about in one's mind. One must have the courage for this. Otherwise one will fail to understand how present-day humanity has developed from a past that was very different.

We are really living in an age now where the present way of living through sleep, waking and dreaming leads to inner conflict in many different ways for anyone who is able to practise self-observation, and above all self-determination. Just as that deep sleep crumbled away from humanity, a sleep that had held so much significance for people in past ages, when the initiate had to explain the nature of what human beings went through in that deep sleep, so does present-day sleep now crumble away. It is not that people would in future dream all night, but they are really going through this stage in such a way that their dreams get duller. In early times they were waking dreams, and these have become our way of having abstract ideas. In the same way the chaotic dreams of today will grow dim and dull and people will have this dull dream sleep. They will not have conscious awareness of the dream. Above this will be the present-day waking stage with abstract thinking called logical. Then, however, there will be a hyper-awareness, and this already comes for those who understand these things. This hyper-awareness concerns itself above all with the human will and with the effect that the will can have as it moves upon the nervous system. If you observe the untrammelled way in which the human will unfolds, doing so in the widest horizons, and understand it, using initiation science, you will see how a heralding of hyper-awareness, a higher form of conscious awareness than the usual waking state of mind, is entering into what souls bring to expression—even going as far as states of physical sickness.

However, people do not yet want to live with this, for they can only experience it if they make spiritual science their own, this spiritual science where one has to think in a very different way from that used in the everyday world, a spiritual science which truly is much more practical than the theoretical life practice of today which is really the most profound non-practice. This spiritual science actually adds a thinking that is inwardly alive to the ordinary abstract way of thinking. This is not something we can add at will and leave aside at will; it is something which results, arises, for a particular organization appears in humanity which did not exist in earlier times. At present we have the first beginnings of it. The blood circulation in man's organs of movement—arms, legs, hands, feet— is progressively changing; man is changing. The condition we often refer to as nervousness today reflects the fact that some kind of higher state wants to enter into man, but man is not yet accepting it. This makes people restless because it is still alien to them. They will only come to rest when they have made it their own.

We can thus see a further three states of mind that lie ahead for humanity, with the human race working its way towards them—a dull dream sleep, a waking state, and being hyper-awake. The reason why so much is shaking and rattling humanity in external life situations is that humanity is resisting, mostly unconsciously, the change that wants to come from spiritual worlds. It will come, however; it wants to come. Above all it does want to get to the human will. Human beings will have to understand in a very different way than they are prepared to do today that when it comes to the spirit, the region has to be passed where protest arises against the laws of nature. Human beings will only come to understand the future, going via the Mystery on Golgotha, if they will be able to rise to the insight that the subject of the Mystery on Golgotha cannot be grasped through natural science, but can be grasped with the power one develops by properly understanding the stage of mere dreaming, which tells of the natural process, and progressing to understanding the other shore of existence. The elements of understanding which are right for future understanding of the Mystery on Golgotha must be gathered from the spiritual shore of existence. It will be essential to position the things which human beings can experience in the present time between the past and the future, and that human beings come to feel themselves to be a transition from this past into the future. They will then also be able to gain more and more understanding for the way of working with spiritual as well as natural truths.

It is easy to understand the error people fall into, for things which are wrong can be so tremendously logical. People fail to consider that things which are wrong can be so tremendously logical. Surely nothing can be more logical than to observe approximately how long some sedimentary rock needs to reach a particular thickness. The most natural way must surely be to calculate that if some geological stratum has such and such a depth, we multiply the small depths with the figure of how many times it fits into the great depth. You will get so and so many years—a geological period was 20 million years, 200 million years ago—Silurian, Devonian or any other. Ah, the calculation is brilliantly correct, nothing to be said against it. Yet what we think is logical does actually deceive us in this case.

This kind of logic always reminds me of the logic which one of the greatest mathematicians of all times[65] once applied to his own life. When he had reached a considerable age he suddenly developed a lung disease. He knew many medical people and through these connections arrived at an idea of how many small abscesses he would have to cough up to get rid of his lung disease. It was a matter of how the lung continues to develop—he arrived at a figure of 15 years. So all would be well in 15 years' time. Only he died two years later. That, you see, is reality. The other thing was logic. That is also how reality relates to logic in the whole of the cosmic universe. It is incredibly easy to prove things, for logic must not be attacked but defended. It has to be expressly said to be correct. It is just as correct as when someone works out, 'My heart goes through a particular process of development. At a certain time it will have reached a particular state. I calculate how long it may take until it reaches this stage: 300 years. I then go back 300 years, working out what my heart was like 300 years ago.' The problem is that as a physical human being I did not live with this physical heart 300 years ago! Nor will I be alive in 300 years' time. The earth also did not exist at the times calculated by geologists, for it needs the spiritual order to perceive what the earth has gone through in the past. That is what is so beguiling about modern science, that things which are illusionary can be so easily proved, but that the proofs tell us nothing about the

truth. Today human beings are therefore living in fear—not consciously so, for they do not wish it, but subconsciously—fear that the
truth must really be lost to them. We see this fear shimmer out from
many things people say today. Essentially those who develop
philosophies of life on the basis of materialism do not feel very
comfortable with them. They feel some anxiety everywhere about
boundaries which they do not want to cross, though on the other
hand these boundaries present terrible obstacles to living a fully
human life. People do have a feeling that if they accept only the
natural order they cannot really live with this, and that above all such
natural order as we take up into our life of ideas cannot lead to
artistic and religious sentience and ideas that have genuine inwardness. We must not forget that the religious system we have today
comes from times when human beings fathomed the cosmic world
out of that deep sleep. All our religious institutions are from those
ancient times. The religious institutions, not the Mystery on Golgotha. That does not depend on any kind of religious view; it is a fact
that has taken its place in earth evolution. This must be grasped also
in the states of mind which are now only in preparation. The religion-
creative faculty of humanity has been unfruitful for many centuries
and indeed millennia; genuine artistic powers have remained
unfruitful. Apart from just a few renaissances we are not really living
in originally elementary creativeness. Yet this wants to come into our
time. And the human discomfort, which is the most marked
phenomenon in our civilization, represents the birth pangs, as it
were, of a new era, a new era on a scientific, a new era on an artistic, a
new era on a social, religious, moral basis, the future of humanity.
This must above all be close to our hearts, for humanity must live
towards that future. At no other time was the human ear less inclined
to hear initiation science. In a way we may also say that at no other
time did humanity have greater need of this than today.

This is the reason why specifically for this conference I wanted to
speak about the past, present and future of man, considering the
development of the human mind. With only three lectures, it had to
be rather sketchy, but individuals can develop the things I have said

further for themselves. It seems to me that the conscious mind, being closest to individual human nature, is also the one thing that will most easily bear fruit for the individual, stimulating him so that he will enter more and more into spiritual experience as such. The people of our time need this kind of spiritual life—not materialistic life—so that they may be the human beings of the future. Because human beings have come to think and form ideas in an abstract, powerless way, I would say all inner ways of life they have developed have become such, for the time being, that with present-day education it really is the case that to speak to them of things of the spirit has the same effect as speaking of logarithm tables to the simple-minded uncle. When mighty signs do after all come up here or there for the desire of the spiritual world to come in, people misinterpret this, as if they were the house numbers of Europe. A slightly far-fetched comparison, but understandable in view of what I have been saying. The general lifestyle, or rather way of judging life, also enters into the most scientific thinking and there turns into not just bourgeois but the lowest form of humanity lacking in all imagination to the nth degree, moral hypocrisy dressed up and embroidered scientifically. If ever something wants to emerge, even just a trace of it, people consider it to be something which from the materialistic point of view and good common sense can only be said to be 'crazy'.

In this case, too, there is a nice story based on reality. In the early 1840s the philosopher Schelling,[66] grown old by then, was called from Munich to Berlin. He had been silent for a long time. A man with a great reputation, he was to present positive philosophy in contrast to negative philosophy—a term he was himself using. His intention was to evolve the development at least of the spiritual life of humanity, the development of the mysteries and of religion, going infinitely deeper at that time at Berlin University than anyone has done even to this day. When Schelling gave his first lecture in Berlin, the most illuminated minds were sitting in the front row, certainly no students but the professors from all faculties, leading educators, the most illustrious representatives of academic life. The students sat at the very back. And the audience was actually waiting—in so far as one could honestly wait there—for the fulfilment to be brought by this man of renown. Yet faces grew longer and longer as Schelling gave his first lecture. He did speak of the spirit in a special way, he spoke of the spirit at a time when the age of materialism was coming to its peak, was just about to be in full flower. He spoke of the spirit. Faces grew longer and longer, and people did not know what he was aiming at. They simply did not know this. The philosopher Trendelenburg,[67] later to be famous, was sitting in those front rows. He said that he thought he had understood a very little of this philosophy, but not the rest, but he was not sure if he had really understood this very little. Now you see, one day one of the people who had heard the lecture met someone else who had also been present. People—including these two—had been cudgelling their brains for days, saying, 'Why was Schelling called to Berlin, seeing that no one can understand the things he says?' Well, the friend was able to tell the other, for he was able to inform him that Schelling's daughter had got engaged to the son of the minister of education. So now it was possible to understand why Schelling wanted to go to Berlin; now the matter made sense.

Yes, it does indeed seem paradoxical when one is telling such things, but one has to put it like this, for anything that can be grasped with the way of thinking which is characteristic of our time is that far removed, for the time being, from something which as spiritual science truly does not point to the future in an arbitrary way but because it is an inner human need, because the human race must fall into decadence unless it gains a new spirituality. This new spirituality alone will be able to experience the three full states of mind which have to be gained in future—subdued dream sleep, the ordinary waking state, and the hyper-awake state. Otherwise human beings will not be able to experience their humanity in future times on earth. For the Godhead wants to develop this future threefold human being from the present threefold human being, just as it developed the present threefold human being—dreaming, sleeping, waking—from the old human being who dreamed in images, slept with an aftertaste on waking, and knew deep sleep. Today, man has arrived in the age of freedom—as I have often explained it for anthroposophists. He has to decide to use his own free powers of insight to live towards that which the Godhead of the world has determined for him.

Then it will be possible not only to think in the present day but above all have the right sentience concerning the past, present and future of man. It will then also be possible to have the will for life on earth to be in accord with what the divine and spiritual world order truly should be from the past, through the present and into the future.

This is what I wanted to say. With these words I wish to end my talk, and only wish in conclusion that tomorrow we shall start such a discussion here[68] that within the Anthroposophical Society it will be evident that there is now a real will to shape this Society in such a way that there will be a real, lively awareness in this Society of what the full human being is meant to be, a full human being who must see himself properly as the human being of the past, the human being of the present, the human being of the future. For these three are also one. And that which man has been in the past, is in the present and shall be in future will one day, I would like to say, encompass the whole *anthropos* before the divine world order. But it will need to be striven for in that an anthroposophy which is taken up enthusiastically, with all one's heart, guides us to the true, genuine *anthropos*, the whole, total human being.

NOTES

Sources. The three lectures in Dornach and the one in London were taken down in shorthand by professional stenographer Helene Finckh; the name of the stenographer who took down the three lectures in Stuttgart is not known. They are here based on the clear text produced by the stenographer.

Titles. The title for the volume in the German edition and those for the lectures were not given by Rudolf Steiner, the exception being the title for the Stuttgart lectures. These were advertised under the title Man in the Past, Present and Future. Otherwise the titles of lectures published earlier were taken from the lectures published by Marie Steiner.

Blackboard drawings. The originals could be preserved by putting sheets of black paper on the boards. They have been published (reduced in size) in vol. XIII of the series *Rudolf Steiner—Wandtafelzeichnungen zum Vortragswerk* (blackboard drawings to Rudolf Steiner's collected lectures). The copies of the drawings from earlier editions have been reproduced in this volume.

Earlier translations. Dornach, 27 July 1923: 'Spiritual Individualities of the Planets' in *The Golden Blade* 1966 and 1988.
London, 2 September 1923: in *The Descent of the Spirit*; *Man as a Picture of the Living Spirit*; *Rudolf Steiner Speaks to the British*.
Dornach, 10 September, Stuttgart, 14, 15 and 16 September 1923: *Man in the Past, the Present and the Future*.

1. *What is Anthroposophy? Three Perspectives on Self-knowledge*, CW 225, three lectures given in Dornach on 20, 21 and 22 July 1923, tr. C. Bamford, M. Spiegler.
2. Vedas (Sanskrit) derived from a word meaning 'to know', the most ancient and sacred literary and religious works of the Hindus, said to be divine in origin. There are four collections of a wisdom which was originally only passed on orally. Vedanta, meaning 'the end (or completion) of the Veda', comprises the most recent of the Vedas, with the term later applied to a number of theological systems in Indian philosophy, initially in the Brahma sutras ascribed to Badarayana (about 200 BC), then the classic Vedanta system of the great philosopher Adi Shankara (AD 788–820).
3. In the 1st German edition the shorthand record of the sentence read as: 'A language gains in inner depth, in soul, when Venus happens to be in quadrature with Mars. On the other hand a language grows soulless, ringing, when

Venus and Mars are in conjunction.' Unfortunately the terms quadrature and conjunction were changed over in the 2nd German edition. In the present, 3rd edition the sentence is again following the shorthand record and thus the same as in the 1st edition.

4. Sir Isaac Newton (1642–1727), English mathematician, physicist and astronomer. In conclusion formulated the principles of classic mechanics and by applying them to celestial phenomena became the founder of celestial mechanics. His principal work was *Philosophiae naturalis principia mathematica* (1687). See also Rudolf Steiner's lectures in Stuttgart on 1–18 January 1921 in *The Relationship of the Diverse Branches of Natural Science to Astronomy* (CW 323, tr. R. Mansell).

5. Kant-Laplace nebular hypothesis derives from Immanuel Kant's nebular hypothesis in his *Universal Natural History and Theory of Heaven* (1755), according to which the earth evolved from a nebula, and—independently of Kant and in many respects deviating from Kant—from the theories in *Exposition du système du monde* (1796) by the mathematician and astronomer Pierre Simon Marquis de Laplace (1749–1827).

6. Monists and other leagues: the German Monist League was established in Jena in 1906, with Ernst Haeckel its Honorary President. The League had among other things links with the Giordano Bruno Bund für einheitliche Weltanschauung (est. 1900), the German Society for Ethical Culture and other reform movements. Rudolf Steiner was a member of the Giordano Bruno League.

7. General theory of relativity formulated by the physicist Albert Einstein (1879–1955) from 1905 onwards. See Rudolf Steiner's *The Riddles of Philosophy*, CW 18, the chapter on 'Modern man and his philosophy of life'.

8. Ponnambalam Ramanathan (1851–1930), Solicitor General of Ceylon [Sri Lanka], *The Culture of the Soul among Western Nationals*, New York and London 1906.

9. Goethe, *Faust I*, Study, words spoken by Mephistopheles.

10. *Pistis Sophia* (Greek 'faith—wisdom'), title of a work ascribed to the Gnostic Valentinus, brought to England by Askew (Codex Askewianus) and first published in Latin in Berlin by Petermann in 1851. The first French edition followed in 1895, the English, by Mead, in 1896, and the German, by Carl Schmidt, in 1905.

11. This lecture (without its conclusion) has also been published in *Colour*, tr. J. Salter, P. Wehrle.

12. Three lectures, given in Dornach on 20–23 July 1923. English edition CW 225, *What is Anthroposophy?* tr. C. Bamford, M. Spiegler, Anthroposophic Press, 2002.

13. Euclid of Megara (around 300 BC), Greek mathematician

14. Antoine Laurent de Lavoisier (1743–94), French chemist. He proposed a new chemical nomenclature in his main work *Traité élémentaire de chimie* (2 volumes, 1789).

15. Cenni di Pepo (c. 1240 to after 1302), Italian painter and mosaicist.

16. Giotto di Bondone (c. 1266 or 1276–1337), Italian painter and architect.

17. Raffaello Santi (1481–1520), Italian painter and architect.

18. From 1915 onwards, programmes for performances at the Goetheanum were illustrated by various painters. This later also led to Rudolf Steiner producing artistic motifs for programme illustrations to which he was referring here. See the art reproductions GA (CW) K 55.1–55.5.

19. Eduard von Hartmann (1842–1906), well-known nineteenth-century philosopher. The quote comes from his *Philosophie des Unbewussten* (Philosophy of the Unconscious), 1869, vol. 2, end of chapter 14. Other works were *Die Religion des Geistes* (The Religion of the Spirit), 1882; *Grundprobleme der Erkenntnistheorie* (Fundamental problems of epistemology), 1889. Detailed information on oral and written communications between Rudolf Steiner and Hartmann may be found in *Dokumente zur Philosophie der Freiheit*, CW 4.

20. As part of a Holiday Conference in Ilkley (Yorkshire) organized by the Educational Union for the Realization of Spiritual Values, Rudolf Steiner gave 14 lectures on 5–17 August 1923, published in *A Modern Art of Education* (CW 307), tr. J. Darrell, G. Adams. His 13 lectures in Penmaenmawr on 18–31 August 1923 have been published in *The Evolution of Consciousness*, CW 307, tr. V.E. Watkin, C. Davy. On 2 September 1923 he spoke in London at the Foundation Meeting of the Anthroposophical Society in Great Britain. Two lectures he gave there for physicians on 2 and 3 September have been published in *The Healing Process* (CW 319), tr. C.E. Creeger. Eight eurythmy performances were given in Ilkley, Penmaenmawr and London under the aegis of Marie Steiner, with Rudolf Steiner giving introductions.

21. The words of farewell concluding this lecture where Rudolf Steiner referred to the rebuilding of the Goetheanum are published in *Rudolf Steiner Speaks to the British*, tr. J. Collis.

22. See Note 20.

23. Lecture given in London on 30 August 1922 has been published in *The Mystery of the Trinity* (from CW 214), tr. not known.

24. See Note 8.

25. Part of this lecture is (in German) included in *Initiations-Erkenntnis* (CW 227), 4th edition 2000 (appendix).

26. See Note 20.

27. In a lecture given in Berlin on 30 September 1904 Rudolf Steiner spoke at length about the mysteries of the Druids and Druhtinaz. Notes on the lecture are included in the volume *The Temple Legend*, CW 93, which also gives details about the Druids and the Scandinavian mysteries from Charles William Heckethorn's *The Secret Societies of All Ages and Countries*. A copy of the German edition of this is in Rudolf Steiner's library, with marks he made in it.

28. Friedrich Froebel (1782–1852), German educationalist. Developed a view on education based on the work of J.H. Pestalozzi, with the emphasis on developing all the human being's capacities. Established his first kindergarten in 1837 and a training college for kindergarten teachers. Also developed Froebel Gifts for play and engagement, e.g. ball, sphere, roller, cube. He published his *The Education of Man* in 1826.

29. See Note 42.

30. Hermann von Baravalle (1898–1973), mathematician and physicist. Teacher

at the Independent Stuttgart Waldorf School from 1920. His book was entitled *Zur Paedagogik der Physik und Mathematik*, Stuttgart 1921.

31. Julie Laemmert (1879–1959), teaching choir singing and creative speech at the Independent Stuttgart Waldorf School.

32. Erich Schwebsch (1889–1953), music writer and educationist. Joined Stuttgart Waldorf School staff in 1921.

33. Caroline von Heydebrand (1886–1938), joined Stuttgart Waldorf School staff in 1919.

34. Karl Schubert (1889–1949). In charge of special needs class at the Stuttgart Waldorf School from 1920.

35. Edith Roehrle (Ritter-) (1893–1965), teacher and eurythmist at Stuttgart Waldorf School 1920–31.

36. Twelve lectures, Oxford, 16–29 August 1922, CW 305: *Oxford Conference on Spiritual Values in Education and Social Life*.

37. See Note 22.

38. Guenther Wachsmuth (1893–1963), on the Council of the General Anthroposophical Society, 1923–1963 secretary, treasurer and head of Science Section, School of Spiritual Science at the Goetheanum. Was accompanying Rudolf Steiner on his journeys at the time.

39. Daniel Dunlop (1868–1935) organized the Summer Schools at Penmaenmawr (1923) and Torquay (1924), established British Weleda company; general secretary of the Anthroposophical Society in England.

40. Margaret McMillan, *Education through the Imagination*, George Allen and Unwin Ltd, London 1923.

41. *Das Goetheanum*, vol. 3 No. 5, 9 September 1923.

42. Margaret McMillan (1860–1931) was a Christian, a socialist and a member of the Fabian Society. She met Rudolf Steiner in 1922 through Millicent Mackenzie.

43. See *Der Lehrerkreis um Rudolf Steiner in der ersten Waldorfschule 1919–1925*, edited by Gisbert Husemann and Johannes Tautz. Verlag Freies Geistesleben, Stuttgart 1977.

44. Ita Wegman (1893–1976) established the Institute of Clinical Medicine in Arlesheim in 1921 and wrote *Extending Practical Medicine* together with Rudolf Steiner.

45. Francis Valiant Larkins, London physician. His wife supported the eurythmy work in London. Rudolf Steiner was staying with them during the days of the course.

46. London, 2 and 3 September 1923, in *The Healing Process* (CW 319), tr. C.E. Creeger.

47. The earthquake which hit Tokyo in 1923, with a death toll of 100,000 and 650,000 buildings destroyed.

48. See also the lecture of 14 August 1908 in *Universe, Earth and Man* (CW 105), tr. M. Cotterell et al.

49. See also Rudolf Steiner's lectures in Berlin on 30 September 1904, notes on which may be found in *The Temple Legend* (CW 93), on 6 May 1909, in *European Mysteries and their Initiates* (CW 57), and in Oslo on 15 June 1910 in *The Mission of the Individual Folk Souls* (CW 121).

50. Old Norse Edda, collection of songs and sayings in Old Norse and Icelandic from the ninth to the twelfth centuries, recorded after 1250, 1st edition Copenhagen 1787–1825. The first song of the Hans Voss edition (in Rudolf Steiner's library) has been summarized in the addenda to the lecture of 30 September 1904 in *The Temple Legend and the Golden Legend* (CW 93).

51. See lecture given in Stuttgart on 8 August 1904 in *Universe, Earth and Man* (CW 105), and details on Baldur spirit and Edda in ref. 50.

52. First lecture at September Conference of Anthroposophical Society in Germany. The introductory words of the Welcome may be found in *Das Schicksalsjahr 1923* (CW 259).

53. John Scotus Erigena (*c.* 800–*c.* 877), translated the writings of Dionysius the Areopagite. Author of *De divina praedestione* and *De divisione naturae*. All his works were condemned to be burned by the Vatican in 1225.

54. René Descartes (1596–1650), French philosopher, mathematician and scientist.

55. See Note 20.

56. Was the Anthroposophical Society's address at that time.

57. Goethe, *Metamorphosis of Plants*, also in CW 1).

58. Jacob Boehme (1575–1624), mystic. See also lecture given in Berlin on 3 May 1906 in German CW 54, not translated, and on 9 January 1913, in Steiner/Barnetson *Jacob Boehme*, CW 62.

59. Emanuel Swedenborg (Swedberg) (1688–1722), Swedish naturalist and theosophist.

60. This may sound strange, but as the original shorthand record is not available we might at most ask if the words were misheard and might have been 'the existence of which we might possibly doubt'.

61. *Mysterium magnum* (1623); *De Signatura rerum* (1622); *Aurora or Day-Spring* (1612).

62. Philippus Theophrastus Bombastus von Hohenheim (1493–1520), physician, naturalist and philosopher.

63. Ludwig Staudenmaier (1865–1933), university professor in Freising nr Munich, *Die Magie als experimentelle Naturwissenschft* (magic as an experimental science), 1912. See also Rudolf Steiner's lecture of 22 September 1923 in Dornach (CW 225).

64. Kuno Fischer (1824–1907), philosophy historian.

65. Leonhard Euler (1707–83).

66. Friedrich Wilhelm Joseph von Schelling (1775–1854).

67. Friedrich Adolf Trendelenburg (1802–72).

68. Refers to a discussion of matters relating to the Anthroposophical Society, Stuttgart, 17 September 1923. No record of this is available.

RUDOLF STEINER'S COLLECTED WORKS

The German Edition of Rudolf Steiner's Collected Works (the *Gesamtausgabe* [GA] published by Rudolf Steiner Verlag, Dornach, Switzerland) presently runs to 354 titles, organized either by type of work (written or spoken), chronology, audience (public or other), or subject (education, art, etc.). For ease of comparison, the Collected Works in English [CW] follows the German organization exactly. A complete listing of the CWs follows with literal translations of the German titles. Other than in the case of the books published in his lifetime, titles were rarely given by Rudolf Steiner himself, and were often provided by the editors of the German editions. The titles in English are not necessarily the same as the German; and, indeed, over the past seventy-five years have frequently been different, with the same book sometimes appearing under different titles.

For ease of identification and to avoid confusion, we suggest that readers looking for a title should do so by CW number. Because the work of creating the Collected Works of Rudolf Steiner is an ongoing process, with new titles being published every year, we have not indicated in this listing which books are presently available. To find out what titles in the Collected Works are currently in print, please check our website at www.rudolfsteinerpress.com (or www.steinerbooks.org for US readers).

Written Work

CW 1	Goethe: Natural-Scientific Writings, Introduction, with Footnotes and Explanations in the text by Rudolf Steiner
CW 2	Outlines of an Epistemology of the Goethean World View, with Special Consideration of Schiller
CW 3	Truth and Science
CW 4	The Philosophy of Freedom
CW 4a	Documents to 'The Philosophy of Freedom'
CW 5	Friedrich Nietzsche, A Fighter against His Time
CW 6	Goethe's Worldview
CW 6a	Now in CW 30
CW 7	Mysticism at the Dawn of Modern Spiritual Life and Its Relationship with Modern Worldviews
CW 8	Christianity as Mystical Fact and the Mysteries of Antiquity
CW 9	Theosophy: An Introduction into Supersensible World Knowledge and Human Purpose
CW 10	How Does One Attain Knowledge of Higher Worlds?
CW 11	From the Akasha-Chronicle

Public Lectures

Lectures to the Members of the Anthroposophical Society

CW 200   The New Spirituality and the Christ-Experience of the 20th Century
CW 201   The Correspondences Between Microcosm and Macrocosm. The Human Being—A Hieroglyph of the Universe. The Human Being in Relationship with the Cosmos: 1
CW 202   The Bridge between the World-Spirituality and the Physical Aspect of the Human Being. The Search for the New Isis, the Divine Sophia. The Human Being in Relationship with the Cosmos: 2
CW 203   The Responsibility of Human Beings for the Development of the World through their Spiritual Connection with the Planet Earth and the World of the Stars. The Human Being in Relationship with the Cosmos: 3
CW 204   Perspectives of the Development of Humanity. The Materialistic Knowledge-Impulse and the Task of Anthroposophy. The Human Being in Relationship with the Cosmos: 4
CW 205   Human Development, World-Soul, and World-Spirit. Part One: The Human Being as a Being of Body and Soul in Relationship to the World. The Human Being in Relationship with the Cosmos: 5
CW 206   Human Development, World-Soul, and World-Spirit. Part Two: The Human Being as a Spiritual Being in the Process of Historical Development. The Human Being in Relationship with the Cosmos: 6
CW 207   Anthroposophy as Cosmosophy. Part One: Characteristic Features of the Human Being in the Earthly and the Cosmic Realms. The Human Being in Relationship with the Cosmos: 7
CW 208   Anthroposophy as Cosmosophy. Part Two: The Forming of the Human Being as the Result of Cosmic Influence. The Human Being in Relationship with the Cosmos: 8
CW 209   Nordic and Central European Spiritual Impulses. The Festival of the Appearance of Christ. The Human Being in Relationship with the Cosmos: 9
CW 210   Old and New Methods of Initiation. Drama and Poetry in the Change of Consciousness in the Modern Age
CW 211   The Sun Mystery and the Mystery of Death and Resurrection. Exoteric and Esoteric Christianity
CW 212   Human Soul Life and Spiritual Striving in Connection with World and Earth Development
CW 213   Human Questions and World Answers
CW 214   The Mystery of the Trinity: The Human Being in Relationship with the Spiritual World in the Course of Time
CW 215   Philosophy, Cosmology, and Religion in Anthroposophy
CW 216   The Fundamental Impulses of the World-Historical Development of Humanity
CW 217   Spiritually Active Forces in the Coexistence of the Older and Younger Generations. Pedagogical Course for Youth

SIGNIFICANT EVENTS IN THE LIFE OF
RUDOLF STEINER

1829:   June 23: birth of Johann Steiner (1829–1910)—Rudolf Steiner's
         father—in Geras, Lower Austria.
1834:   May 8: birth of Franciska Blie (1834–1918)—Rudolf Steiner's mother—
         in Horn, Lower Austria. 'My father and mother were both children of the
         glorious Lower Austrian forest district north of the Danube.'
1860:   May 16: marriage of Johann Steiner and Franciska Blie.
1861:   February 25: birth of *Rudolf Joseph Lorenz Steiner* in Kraljevec, Croatia,
         near the border with Hungary, where Johann Steiner works as a tele-
         grapher for the South Austria Railroad. Rudolf Steiner is baptized two
         days later, February 27, the date usually given as his birthday.
1862:   Summer: the family moves to Mödling, Lower Austria.
1863:   The family moves to Pottschach, Lower Austria, near the Styrian border,
         where Johann Steiner becomes stationmaster. 'The view stretched to the
         mountains ... majestic peaks in the distance and the sweet charm of
         nature in the immediate surroundings.'
1864:   November 15: birth of Rudolf Steiner's sister, Leopoldine (d. November
         1, 1927). She will become a seamstress and live with her parents for the
         rest of her life.
1866:   July 28: birth of Rudolf Steiner's deaf-mute brother, Gustav (d. May 1,
         1941).
1867:   Rudolf Steiner enters the village school. Following a disagreement
         between his father and the schoolmaster, whose wife falsely accused the
         boy of causing a commotion, Rudolf Steiner is taken out of school and
         taught at home.
1868:   A critical experience. Unknown to the family, an aunt dies in a distant
         town. Sitting in the station waiting room, Rudolf Steiner sees her 'form,'
         which speaks to him, asking for help. 'Beginning with this experience, a
         new soul life began in the boy, one in which not only the outer trees and
         mountains spoke to him, but also the worlds that lay behind them. From
         this moment on, the boy began to live with the spirits of nature ...'
1869:   The family moves to the peaceful, rural village of Neudörfl, near Wiener-
         Neustadt in present-day Austria. Rudolf Steiner attends the village
         school. Because of the 'unorthodoxy' of his writing and spelling, he has to
         do 'extra lessons.'
1870:   Through a book lent to him by his tutor, he discovers geometry: 'To
         grasp something purely in the spirit brought me inner happiness. I know
         that I first learned happiness through geometry.' The same tutor allows

him to draw, while other students still struggle with their reading and writing. 'An artistic element' thus enters his education.

1871: Though his parents are not religious, Rudolf Steiner becomes a 'church child,' a favourite of the priest, who was 'an exceptional character.' 'Up to the age of ten or eleven, among those I came to know, he was far and away the most significant.' Among other things, he introduces Steiner to Copernican, heliocentric cosmology. As an altar boy, Rudolf Steiner serves at Masses, funerals, and Corpus Christi processions. At year's end, after an incident in which he escapes a thrashing, his father forbids him to go to church.

1872: Rudolf Steiner transfers to grammar school in Wiener-Neustadt, a five-mile walk from home, which must be done in all weathers.

1873–75: Through his teachers and on his own, Rudolf Steiner has many wonderful experiences with science and mathematics. Outside school, he teaches himself analytic geometry, trigonometry, differential equations, and calculus.

1876: Rudolf Steiner begins tutoring other students. He learns bookbinding from his father. He also teaches himself stenography.

1877: Rudolf Steiner discovers Kant's *Critique of Pure Reason*, which he reads and rereads. He also discovers and reads von Rotteck's *World History*.

1878: He studies extensively in contemporary psychology and philosophy.

1879: Rudolf Steiner graduates from high school with honours. His father is transferred to Inzersdorf, near Vienna. He uses his first visit to Vienna 'to purchase a great number of philosophy books'—Kant, Fichte, Schelling, and Hegel, as well as numerous histories of philosophy. His aim: to find a path from the 'I' to nature.

October 1879–1883: Rudolf Steiner attends the Technical College in Vienna—to study mathematics, chemistry, physics, mineralogy, botany, zoology, biology, geology, and mechanics—with a scholarship. He also attends lectures in history and literature, while avidly reading philosophy on his own. His two favourite professors are Karl Julius Schröer (German language and literature) and Edmund Reitlinger (physics). He also audits lectures by Robert Zimmermann on aesthetics and Franz Brentano on philosophy. During this year he begins his friendship with Moritz Zitter (1861–1921), who will help support him financially when he is in Berlin.

1880: Rudolf Steiner attends lectures on Schiller and Goethe by Karl Julius Schröer, who becomes his mentor. Also 'through a remarkable combination of circumstances,' he meets Felix Koguzki, a 'herb gatherer' and healer, who could 'see deeply into the secrets of nature.' Rudolf Steiner will meet and study with this 'emissary of the Master' throughout his time in Vienna.

1881: January: '... I didn't sleep a wink. I was busy with philosophical problems until about 12:30 a.m. Then, finally, I threw myself down on my couch. All my striving during the previous year had been to research whether the following statement by Schelling was true or not: *Within everyone dwells a secret, marvelous capacity to draw back from the stream of time—out of the self clothed in all that comes to us from outside—into our innermost being and there, in the immutable form of the Eternal, to look into ourselves.* I believe, and I am still quite certain of it, that I discovered this capacity in myself; I had long had an inkling of it. Now the whole of idealist philosophy stood before me in modified form. What's a sleepless night compared to that!'

Rudolf Steiner begins communicating with leading thinkers of the day, who send him books in return, which he reads eagerly.

July: 'I am not one of those who dives into the day like an animal in human form. I pursue a quite specific goal, an idealistic aim—knowledge of the truth! This cannot be done offhandedly. It requires the greatest striving in the world, free of all egotism, and equally of all resignation.'

August: Steiner puts down on paper for the first time thoughts for a 'Philosophy of Freedom.' 'The striving for the absolute: this human yearning is freedom.' He also seeks to outline a 'peasant philosophy,' describing what the worldview of a 'peasant'—one who lives close to the earth and the old ways—really is.

1881–1882: Felix Koguzki, the herb gatherer, reveals himself to be the envoy of another, higher initiatory personality, who instructs Rudolf Steiner to penetrate Fichte's philosophy and to master modern scientific thinking as a preparation for right entry into the spirit. This 'Master' also teaches him the double (evolutionary and involutionary) nature of time.

1882: Through the offices of Karl Julius Schröer, Rudolf Steiner is asked by Joseph Kürschner to edit Goethe's scientific works for the *Deutschen National-Literatur* edition. He writes 'A Possible Critique of Atomistic Concepts' and sends it to Friedrich Theodor Vischer.

1883: Rudolf Steiner completes his college studies and begins work on the Goethe project.

1884: First volume of Goethe's *Scientific Writings* (CW 1) appears (March). He lectures on Goethe and Lessing, and Goethe's approach to science. In July, he enters the household of Ladislaus and Pauline Specht as tutor to the four Specht boys. He will live there until 1890. At this time, he meets Josef Breuer (1842–1925), the co-author with Sigmund Freud of *Studies in Hysteria*, who is the Specht family doctor.

1885: While continuing to edit Goethe's writings, Rudolf Steiner reads deeply in contemporary philosophy (Eduard von Hartmann, Johannes Volkelt, and Richard Wahle, among others).

1886: May: Rudolf Steiner sends Kürschner the manuscript of *Outlines of Goethe's Theory of Knowledge* (CW 2), which appears in October, and which he sends out widely. He also meets the poet Marie Eugenie Delle Grazie and writes 'Nature and Our Ideals' for her. He attends her salon, where he meets many priests, theologians, and philosophers, who will become his friends. Meanwhile, the director of the Goethe Archive in Weimar requests his collaboration with the *Sophien* edition of Goethe's works, particularly the writings on colour.

1887: At the beginning of the year, Rudolf Steiner is very sick. As the year progresses and his health improves, he becomes increasingly 'a man of letters,' lecturing, writing essays, and taking part in Austrian cultural life. In August–September, the second volume of Goethe's *Scientific Writings* appears.

1888:   January–July: Rudolf Steiner assumes editorship of the 'German Weekly' (*Deutsche Wochenschrift*). He begins lecturing more intensively, giving, for example, a lecture titled 'Goethe as Father of a New Aesthetics.' He meets and becomes soul friends with Friedrich Eckstein (1861–1939), a vegetarian, philosopher of symbolism, alchemist, and musician, who will introduce him to various spiritual currents (including Theosophy) and with whom he will meditate and interpret esoteric and alchemical texts.

1889:   Rudolf Steiner first reads Nietzsche (*Beyond Good and Evil*). He encounters Theosophy again and learns of Madame Blavatsky in the Theosophical circle around Marie Lang (1858–1934). Here he also meets well-known figures of Austrian life, as well as esoteric figures like the occultist Franz Hartmann and Karl Leinigen-Billigen (translator of C.G. Harrison's *The Transcendental Universe*). During this period, Steiner first reads A.P. Sinnett's *Esoteric Buddhism* and Mabel Collins's *Light on the Path*. He also begins travelling, visiting Budapest, Weimar, and Berlin (where he meets philosopher Eduard von Hartmann).

1890:   Rudolf Steiner finishes volume 3 of Goethe's scientific writings. He begins his doctoral dissertation, which will become *Truth and Science* (CW 3). He also meets the poet and feminist Rosa Mayreder (1858–1938), with whom he can exchange his most intimate thoughts. In September, Rudolf Steiner moves to Weimar to work in the Goethe-Schiller Archive.

1891:   Volume 3 of the Kürschner edition of Goethe appears. Meanwhile, Rudolf Steiner edits Goethe's studies in mineralogy and scientific writings for the *Sophien* edition. He meets Ludwig Laistner of the Cotta Publishing Company, who asks for a book on the basic question of metaphysics. From this will result, ultimately, *The Philosophy of Freedom* (CW 4), which will be published not by Cotta but by Emil Felber. In October, Rudolf Steiner takes the oral exam for a doctorate in philosophy, mathematics, and mechanics at Rostock University, receiving his doctorate on the twenty-sixth. In November, he gives his first lecture on Goethe's 'Fairy Tale' in Vienna.

1892:   Rudolf Steiner continues work at the Goethe-Schiller Archive and on his *Philosophy of Freedom*. *Truth and Science*, his doctoral dissertation, is published. Steiner undertakes to write introductions to books on Schopenhauer and Jean Paul for Cotta. At year's end, he finds lodging with Anna Eunike, née Schulz (1853–1911), a widow with four daughters and a son. He also develops a friendship with Otto Erich Hartleben (1864–1905) with whom he shares literary interests.

1893:   Rudolf Steiner begins his habit of producing many reviews and articles. In March, he gives a lecture titled 'Hypnotism, with Reference to Spiritism.' In September, volume 4 of the Kürschner edition is completed. In November, *The Philosophy of Freedom* appears. This year, too, he meets John Henry Mackay (1864–1933), the anarchist, and Max Stirner, a scholar and biographer.

1894:   Rudolf Steiner meets Elisabeth Förster Nietzsche, the philosopher's sister, and begins to read Nietzsche in earnest, beginning with the as yet unpublished *Antichrist*. He also meets Ernst Haeckel (1834–1919). In the fall, he begins to write *Nietzsche, A Fighter against His Time* (CW 5).

1895:   May, *Nietzsche, A Fighter against His Time* appears.

1896:   January 22: Rudolf Steiner sees Friedrich Nietzsche for the first and only time. Moves between the Nietzsche and the Goethe-Schiller Archives, where he completes his work before year's end. He falls out with Elisabeth Förster Nietzsche, thus ending his association with the Nietzsche Archive.

1897:   Rudolf Steiner finishes the manuscript of *Goethe's Worldview* (CW 6). He moves to Berlin with Anna Eunike and begins editorship of the *Magazin für Literatur*. From now on, Steiner will write countless reviews, literary and philosophical articles, and so on. He begins lecturing at the 'Free Literary Society.' In September, he attends the Zionist Congress in Basel. He sides with Dreyfus in the Dreyfus affair.

1898:   Rudolf Steiner is very active as an editor in the political, artistic, and theatrical life of Berlin. He becomes friendly with John Henry Mackay and poet Ludwig Jacobowski (1868–1900). He joins Jacobowski's circle of writers, artists, and scientists—'The Coming Ones' (*Die Kommenden*)—and contributes lectures to the group until 1903. He also lectures at the 'League for College Pedagogy.' He writes an article for Goethe's sesquicentennial, 'Goethe's Secret Revelation,' on the 'Fairy Tale of the Green Snake and the Beautiful Lily.'

1898–99: 'This was a trying time for my soul as I looked at Christianity. . . . I was able to progress only by contemplating, by means of spiritual perception, the evolution of Christianity. . . . Conscious knowledge of real Christianity began to dawn in me around the turn of the century. This seed continued to develop. My soul trial occurred shortly before the beginning of the twentieth century. It was decisive for my soul's development that I stood spiritually before the Mystery of Golgotha in a deep and solemn celebration of knowledge.'

1899:   Rudolf Steiner begins teaching and giving lectures and lecture cycles at the Workers' College, founded by Wilhelm Liebknecht (1826–1900). He will continue to do so until 1904. Writes: *Literature and Spiritual Life in the Nineteenth Century; Individualism in Philosophy; Haeckel and His Opponents; Poetry in the Present;* and begins what will become (fifteen years later) *The Riddles of Philosophy* (CW 18). He also meets many artists and writers, including Käthe Kollwitz, Stefan Zweig, and Rainer Maria Rilke. On October 31, he marries Anna Eunike.

1900:   'I thought that the turn of the century must bring humanity a new light. It seemed to me that the separation of human thinking and willing from the spirit had peaked. A turn or reversal of direction in human evolution seemed to me a necessity.' Rudolf Steiner finishes *World and Life Views in the Nineteenth Century* (the second part of what will become *The Riddles of Philosophy*) and dedicates it to Ernst Haeckel. It is published in March. He continues lecturing at *Die Kommenden*, whose leadership he assumes after the death of Jacobowski. Also, he gives the Gutenberg Jubilee lecture before 7,000 typesetters and printers. In September, Rudolf Steiner is invited by Count and Countess Brockdorff to lecture in the Theosophical Library. His first lecture is on Nietzsche. His second lecture is titled 'Goethe's Secret Revelation.' October 6, he begins a lecture cycle on the mystics that will become *Mystics after Modernism* (CW 7). November–December: 'Marie von Sivers appears in the audience....' Also in November, Steiner gives his first lecture at the Giordano Bruno Bund (where he will continue to lecture until May, 1905). He speaks on Bruno and modern Rome, focusing on the importance of the philosophy of Thomas Aquinas as monism.

1901:   In continual financial straits, Rudolf Steiner's early friends Moritz Zitter and Rosa Mayreder help support him. In October, he begins the lecture cycle *Christianity as Mystical Fact* (CW 8) at the Theosophical Library. In November, he gives his first 'Theosophical lecture' on Goethe's 'Fairy Tale' in Hamburg at the invitation of Wilhelm Hubbe-Schleiden. He also attends a gathering to celebrate the founding of the Theosophical Society at Count and Countess Brockdorff's. He gives a lecture cycle, 'From Buddha to Christ,' for the circle of the *Kommenden*. November 17, Marie von Sivers asks Rudolf Steiner if Theosophy needs a Western-Christian spiritual movement (to complement Theosophy's Eastern emphasis). 'The question was posed. Now, following spiritual laws, I could begin to give an answer....' In December, Rudolf Steiner writes his first article for a Theosophical publication. At year's end, the Brockdorffs and possibly Wilhelm Hubbe-Schleiden ask Rudolf Steiner to join the Theosophical Society and undertake the leadership of the German section. Rudolf Steiner agrees, on the condition that Marie von Sivers (then in Italy) work with him.

1902:   Beginning in January, Rudolf Steiner attends the opening of the Workers' School in Spandau with Rosa Luxemburg (1870–1919). January 17, Rudolf Steiner joins the Theosophical Society. In April, he is asked to become general secretary of the German Section of the Theosophical Society, and works on preparations for its founding. In July, he visits London for a Theosophical congress. He meets Bertram Keightly, G.R.S. Mead, A.P. Sinnett, and Annie Besant, among others. In September, *Christianity as Mystical Fact* appears. In October, Rudolf Steiner gives his first public lecture on Theosophy ('Monism and Theosophy') to about three hundred people at the Giordano Bruno Bund. On October 19–21, the German Section of the Theosophical Society has its first meeting; Rudolf Steiner is the general secretary, and Annie Besant attends. Steiner lectures on practical karma studies. On October 23, Annie Besant inducts Rudolf Steiner into the Esoteric School of the Theosophical Society. On October 25, Steiner begins a weekly series of lectures: 'The Field of Theosophy.' During this year, Rudolf Steiner also first meets Ita Wegman (1876–1943), who will become his close collaborator in his final years.

1903:   Rudolf Steiner holds about 300 lectures and seminars. In May, the first issue of the periodical *Luzifer* appears. In June, Rudolf Steiner visits

London for the first meeting of the Federation of the European Sections of the Theosophical Society, where he meets Colonel Olcott. He begins to write *Theosophy* (CW 9).

1904: Rudolf Steiner continues lecturing at the Workers' College and elsewhere (about 90 lectures), while lecturing intensively all over Germany among Theosophists (about 140 lectures). In February, he meets Carl Unger (1878–1929), who will become a member of the board of the Anthroposophical Society (1913). In March, he meets Michael Bauer (1871–1929), a Christian mystic, who will also be on the board. In May, *Theosophy* appears, with the dedication: 'To the spirit of Giordano Bruno.' Rudolf Steiner and Marie von Sivers visit London for meetings with Annie Besant. June: Rudolf Steiner and Marie von Sivers attend the meeting of the Federation of European Sections of the Theosophical Society in Amsterdam. In July, Steiner begins the articles in *Luzifer-Gnosis* that will become *How to Know Higher Worlds* (CW 10) and *Cosmic Memory* (CW 11). In September, Annie Besant visits Germany. In December, Steiner lectures on Freemasonry. He mentions the High Grade Masonry derived from John Yarker and represented by Theodore Reuss and Karl Kellner as a blank slate 'into which a good image could be placed.'

1905: This year, Steiner ends his non-Theosophical lecturing activity. Supported by Marie von Sivers, his Theosophical lecturing—both in public and in the Theosophical Society—increases significantly: 'The German Theosophical Movement is of exceptional importance.' Steiner recommends reading, among others, Fichte, Jacob Boehme, and Angelus Silesius. He begins to introduce Christian themes into Theosophy. He also begins to work with doctors (Felix Peipers and Ludwig Noll). In July, he is in London for the Federation of European Sections, where he attends a lecture by Annie Besant: 'I have seldom seen Mrs. Besant speak in so inward and heartfelt a manner....' 'Through Mrs. Besant I have found the way to H.P. Blavatsky.' September to October, he gives a course of thirty-one lectures for a small group of esoteric students. In October, the annual meeting of the German Section of the Theosophical Society, which still remains very small, takes place. Rudolf Steiner reports membership has risen from 121 to 377 members. In November, seeking to establish esoteric 'continuity,' Rudolf Steiner and Marie von Sivers participate in a 'Memphis-Misraim' Masonic ceremony. They pay forty-five marks for membership. 'Yesterday, you saw how little remains of former esoteric institutions.' 'We are dealing only with a "framework".... for the present, nothing lies behind it. The occult powers have completely withdrawn.'

1906: Expansion of Theosophical work. Rudolf Steiner gives about 245 lectures, only 44 of which take place in Berlin. Cycles are given in Paris, Leipzig, Stuttgart, and Munich. Esoteric work also intensifies. Rudolf Steiner begins writing *An Outline of Esoteric Science* (CW 13). In January, Rudolf Steiner receives permission (a patent) from the Great Orient of the Scottish A & A Thirty-Three Degree Rite of the Order of the Ancient

Freemasons of the Memphis-Misraim Rite to direct a chapter under the name 'Mystica Aeterna.' This will become the 'Cognitive-Ritual Section' (also called 'Misraim Service') of the Esoteric School. (See: *Freemasonry and Ritual Work: The Misraim Service*, CW 265). During this time, Steiner also meets Albert Schweitzer. In May, he is in Paris, where he visits Edouard Schuré. Many Russians attend his lectures (including Konstantin Balmont, Dimitri Mereszkovski, Zinaida Hippius, and Maximilian Woloshin). He attends the General Meeting of the European Federation of the Theosophical Society, at which Col. Olcott is present for the last time. He spends the year's end in Venice and Rome, where he writes and works on his translation of H.P. Blavatsky's *Key to Theosophy*.

1907:   Further expansion of the German Theosophical Movement according to the Rosicrucian directive to 'introduce spirit into the world'—in education, in social questions, in art, and in science. In February, Col. Olcott dies in Adyar. Before he dies, Olcott indicates that 'the Masters' wish Annie Besant to succeed him: much politicking ensues. Rudolf Steiner supports Besant's candidacy. April-May: preparations for the Congress of the Federation of European Sections of the Theosophical Society—the great, watershed Whitsun 'Munich Congress,' attended by Annie Besant and others. Steiner decides to separate Eastern and Western (Christian-Rosicrucian) esoteric schools. He takes his esoteric school out of the Theosophical Society (Besant and Rudolf Steiner are 'in harmony' on this). Steiner makes his first lecture tours to Austria and Hungary. That summer, he is in Italy. In September, he visits Edouard Schuré, who will write the introduction to the French edition of *Christianity as Mystical Fact* in Barr, Alsace. Rudolf Steiner writes the autobiographical statement known as the 'Barr Document.' In *Luzifer-Gnosis*, 'The Education of the Child' appears.

1908:   The movement grows (membership: 1,150). Lecturing expands. Steiner makes his first extended lecture tour to Holland and Scandinavia, as well as visits to Naples and Sicily. Themes: St. John's Gospel, the Apocalypse, Egypt, science, philosophy, and logic. *Luzifer-Gnosis* ceases publication. In Berlin, Marie von Sivers (with Johanna Mücke (1864–1949) forms the *Philosophisch-Theosophisch* (after 1915 *Philosophisch-Anthroposophisch*) *Verlag* to publish Steiner's work. Steiner gives lecture cycles titled *The Gospel of St. John* (CW 103) and *The Apocalypse* (104).

1909:   *An Outline of Esoteric Science* appears. Lecturing and travel continues. Rudolf Steiner's spiritual research expands to include the polarity of Lucifer and Ahriman; the work of great individualities in history; the Maitreya Buddha and the Bodhisattvas; spiritual economy (CW 109); the work of the spiritual hierarchies in heaven and on earth (CW 110). He also deepens and intensifies his research into the Gospels, giving lectures on the Gospel of St. Luke (CW 114) with the first mention of two Jesus children. Meets and becomes friends with Christian Morgenstern (1871–1914). In April, he lays the foundation stone for the Malsch model—the building that will lead to the first Goetheanum. In May, the International Congress of the Federation of European Sections of the

Theosophical Society takes place in Budapest. Rudolf Steiner receives the
Subba Row medal for *How to Know Higher Worlds*. During this time,
Charles W. Leadbeater discovers Jiddu Krishnamurti (1895–1986) and
proclaims him the future 'world teacher,' the bearer of the Maitreya
Buddha and the 'reappearing Christ.' In October, Steiner delivers
seminal lectures on 'anthroposophy,' which he will try, unsuccessfully, to
rework over the next years into the unfinished work, *Anthroposophy (A
Fragment)* (CW 45).

1910:   New themes: *The Reappearance of Christ in the Etheric* (CW 118); *The Fifth
Gospel; The Mission of Folk Souls* (CW 121); *Occult History* (CW 126); the
evolving development of etheric cognitive capacities. Rudolf Steiner
continues his Gospel research with *The Gospel of St. Matthew* (CW 123). In
January, his father dies. In April, he takes a month-long trip to Italy,
including Rome, Monte Cassino, and Sicily. He also visits Scandinavia
again. July–August, he writes the first mystery drama, *The Portal of
Initiation* (CW 14). In November, he gives 'psychosophy' lectures. In
December, he submits 'On the Psychological Foundations and Episte-
mological Framework of Theosophy' to the International Philosophical
Congress in Bologna.

1911:   The crisis in the Theosophical Society deepens. In January, 'The Order of
the Rising Sun,' which will soon become 'The Order of the Star in the
East,' is founded for the coming world teacher, Krishnamurti. At the
same time, Marie von Sivers, Rudolf Steiner's co-worker, falls ill. Fewer
lectures are given, but important new ground is broken. In Prague, in
March, Steiner meets Franz Kafka (1883–1924) and Hugo Bergmann
(1883-1975). In April, he delivers his paper to the Philosophical Congress. He writes the second mystery drama, *The Soul's Probation* (CW 14).
Also, while Marie von Sivers is convalescing, Rudolf Steiner begins work
on *Calendar 1912/1913*, which will contain the 'Calendar of the Soul'
meditations. On March 19, Anna (Eunike) Steiner dies. In September,
Rudolf Steiner visits Einsiedeln, birthplace of Paracelsus. In December,
Friedrich Rittelmeyer, future founder of the Christian Community, meets
Rudolf Steiner. The *Johannes-Bauverein*, the 'building committee,' which
would lead to the first Goetheanum (first planned for Munich), is also
founded, and a preliminary committee for the founding of an independent association is created that, in the following year, will become the
Anthroposophical Society. Important lecture cycles include *Occult Phy-
siology* (CW 128); *Wonders of the World* (CW 129); *From Jesus to Christ*
(CW 131). Other themes: esoteric Christianity; Christian Rosenkreutz;
the spiritual guidance of humanity; the sense world and the world of the
spirit.

1912:   Despite the ongoing, now increasing crisis in the Theosophical Society,
much is accomplished: *Calendar 1912/1913* is published; eurythmy is
created; both the third mystery drama, *The Guardian of the Threshold* (CW
14) and *A Way of Self-Knowledge* (CW 16) are written. New (or renewed)
themes included life between death and rebirth and karma and
reincarnation. Other lecture cycles: *Spiritual Beings in the Heavenly Bodies*

and in the Kingdoms of Nature (CW 136); *The Human Being in the Light of Occultism, Theosophy, and Philosophy* (CW 137); *The Gospel of St. Mark* (CW 139); and *The Bhagavad Gita and the Epistles of Paul* (CW 142). On May 8, Rudolf Steiner celebrates White Lotus Day, H.P. Blavatsky's death day, which he had faithfully observed for the past decade, for the last time. In August, Rudolf Steiner suggests the 'independent association' be called the 'Anthroposophical Society.' In September, the first eurythmy course takes place. In October, Rudolf Steiner declines recognition of a Theosophical Society lodge dedicated to the Star of the East and decides to expel all Theosophical Society members belonging to the order. Also, with Marie von Sivers, he first visits Dornach, near Basel, Switzerland, and they stand on the hill where the Goetheanum will be built. In November, a Theosophical Society lodge is opened by direct mandate from Adyar (Annie Besant). In December, a meeting of the German section occurs at which it is decided that belonging to the Order of the Star of the East is incompatible with membership in the Theosophical Society. December 28: informal founding of the Anthroposophical Society in Berlin.

1913:   Expulsion of the German section from the Theosophical Society. February 2–3: Foundation meeting of the Anthroposophical Society. Board members include: Marie von Sivers, Michael Bauer, and Carl Unger. September 20: Laying of the foundation stone for the *Johannes Bau* (Goetheanum) in Dornach. Building begins immediately. The third mystery drama, *The Soul's Awakening* (CW 14), is completed. Also: *The Threshold of the Spiritual World* (CW 147). Lecture cycles include: *The Bhagavad Gita and the Epistles of Paul* and *The Esoteric Meaning of the Bhagavad Gita* (CW 146), which the Russian philosopher Nikolai Berdyaev attends; *The Mysteries of the East and of Christianity* (CW 144); *The Effects of Esoteric Development* (CW 145); and *The Fifth Gospel* (CW 148). In May, Rudolf Steiner is in London and Paris, where anthroposophical work continues.

1914:   Building continues on the *Johannes Bau* (Goetheanum) in Dornach, with artists and co-workers from seventeen nations. The general assembly of the Anthroposophical Society takes place. In May, Rudolf Steiner visits Paris, as well as Chartres Cathedral. June 28: assassination in Sarajevo ('Now the catastrophe has happened!'). August 1: War is declared. Rudolf Steiner returns to Germany from Dornach—he will travel back and forth. He writes the last chapter of *The Riddles of Philosophy*. Lecture cycles include: *Human and Cosmic Thought* (CW 151); *Inner Being of Humanity between Death and a New Birth* (CW 153); *Occult Reading and Occult Hearing* (CW 156). December 24: marriage of Rudolf Steiner and Marie von Sivers.

1915:   Building continues. Life after death becomes a major theme, also art. Writes: *Thoughts during a Time of War* (CW 24). Lectures include: *The Secret of Death* (CW 159); *The Uniting of Humanity through the Christ Impulse* (CW 165).

1916:   Rudolf Steiner begins work with Edith Maryon (1872–1924) on the sculpture 'The Representative of Humanity' ('The Group'—Christ, Lucifer, and Ahriman). He also works with the alchemist Alexander von Bernus on the quarterly *Das Reich*. He writes *The Riddle of Humanity* (CW 20). Lectures include: *Necessity and Freedom in World History and Human Action* (CW 166); *Past and Present in the Human Spirit* (CW 167); *The Karma of Vocation* (CW 172); *The Karma of Untruthfulness* (CW 173).

1917:   Russian Revolution. The U.S. enters the war. Building continues. Rudolf Steiner delineates the idea of the 'threefold nature of the human being' (in a public lecture March 15) and the 'threefold nature of the social organism' (hammered out in May–June with the help of Otto von Lerchenfeld and Ludwig Polzer-Hoditz in the form of two documents titled *Memoranda*, which were distributed in high places). August–September: Rudolf Steiner writes *The Riddles of the Soul* (CW 20). Also: commentary on 'The Chymical Wedding of Christian Rosenkreutz' for Alexander Bernus (*Das Reich*). Lectures include: *The Karma of Materialism* (CW 176); *The Spiritual Background of the Outer World: The Fall of the Spirits of Darkness* (CW 177).

1918:   March 18: peace treaty of Brest-Litovsk—'Now everything will truly enter chaos! What is needed is cultural renewal.' June: Rudolf Steiner visits Karlstein (Grail) Castle outside Prague. Lecture cycle: *From Symptom to Reality in Modern History* (CW 185). In mid-November, Emil Molt, of the Waldorf-Astoria Cigarette Company, has the idea of founding a school for his workers' children.

1919:   Focus on the threefold social organism: tireless travel, countless lectures, meetings, and publications. At the same time, a new public stage of Anthroposophy emerges as cultural renewal begins. The coming years will see initiatives in pedagogy, medicine, pharmacology, and agriculture. January 27: threefold meeting: ' We must first of all, with the money we have, found free schools that can bring people what they need.' February: first public eurythmy performance in Zurich. Also: 'Appeal to the German People' (CW 24), circulated March 6 as a newspaper insert. In April, *Towards Social Renewal* (CW 23) appears— 'perhaps the most widely read of all books on politics appearing since the war.' Rudolf Steiner is asked to undertake the 'direction and leadership' of the school founded by the Waldorf-Astoria Company. Rudolf Steiner begins to talk about the 'renewal' of education. May 30: a building is selected and purchased for the future Waldorf School. August–September, Rudolf Steiner gives a lecture course for Waldorf teachers, *The Foundations of Human Experience (Study of Man)* (CW 293). September 7: Opening of the first Waldorf School. December (into January): first science course, the *Light Course* (CW 320).

1920:   The Waldorf School flourishes. New threefold initiatives. Founding of limited companies *Der Kommende Tag* and *Futurum A.G.* to infuse spiritual values into the economic realm. Rudolf Steiner also focuses on the sciences. Lectures: *Introducing Anthroposophical Medicine* (CW 312); *The Warmth Course* (CW 321); *The Boundaries of Natural Science* (CW 322); *The Redemption of Thinking* (CW 74). February: Johannes Werner

Klein—later a co-founder of the Christian Community—asks Rudolf Steiner about the possibility of a 'religious renewal,' a 'Johannine church.' In March, Rudolf Steiner gives the first course for doctors and medical students. In April, a divinity student asks Rudolf Steiner a second time about the possibility of religious renewal. September 27–October 16: anthroposophical 'university course.' December: lectures titled *The Search for the New Isis* (CW 202).

1921: Rudolf Steiner continues his intensive work on cultural renewal, including the uphill battle for the threefold social order. 'University' arts, scientific, theological, and medical courses include: *The Astronomy Course* (CW 323); *Observation, Mathematics, and Scientific Experiment* (CW 324); the *Second Medical Course* (CW 313); *Colour*. In June and September–October, Rudolf Steiner also gives the first two 'priests' courses' (CW 342 and 343). The 'youth movement' gains momentum. Magazines are founded: *Die Drei* (January), and—under the editorship of Albert Steffen (1884–1963)—the weekly, *Das Goetheanum* (August). In February–March, Rudolf Steiner takes his first trip outside Germany since the war (Holland). On April 7, Steiner receives a letter regarding 'religious renewal,' and May 22–23, he agrees to address the question in a practical way. In June, the Klinical-Therapeutic Institute opens in Arlesheim under the direction of Dr. Ita Wegman. In August, the Chemical-Pharmaceutical Laboratory opens in Arlesheim (Oskar Schmiedel and Ita Wegman are directors). The Clinical Therapeutic Institute is inaugurated in Stuttgart (Dr. Ludwig Noll is director); also the Research Laboratory in Dornach (Ehrenfried Pfeiffer and Günther Wachsmuth are directors). In November–December, Rudolf Steiner visits Norway.

1922: The first half of the year involves very active public lecturing (thousands attend); in the second half, Rudolf Steiner begins to withdraw and turn toward the Society—'The Society is asleep.' It is 'too weak' to do what is asked of it. The businesses—*Der Kommende Tag* and *Futurum A.G.*—fail. In January, with the help of an agent, Steiner undertakes a twelve-city German lecture tour, accompanied by eurythmy performances. In two weeks he speaks to more than 2,000 people. In April, he gives a 'university course' in The Hague. He also visits England. In June, he is in Vienna for the East–West Congress. In August–September, he is back in England for the Oxford Conference on Education. Returning to Dornach, he gives the lectures *Philosophy, Cosmology, and Religion* (CW 215), and gives the third priests' course (CW 344). On September 16, The Christian Community is founded. In October–November, Steiner is in Holland and England. He also speaks to the youth: *The Youth Course* (CW 217). In December, Steiner gives lectures titled *The Origins of Natural Science* (CW 326), and *Humanity and the World of Stars: The Spiritual Communion of Humanity* (CW 219). December 31: Fire at the Goetheanum, which is destroyed.

1923: Despite the fire, Rudolf Steiner continues his work unabated. A very hard year. Internal dispersion, dissension, and apathy abound. There is conflict—between old and new visions—within the Society. A wake-up call is needed, and Rudolf Steiner responds with renewed lecturing vitality. His focus: the spiritual context of human life; initiation science; the course of the year; and community building. As a foundation for an artistic school, he creates a series of pastel sketches. Lecture cycles: *The Anthroposophical Movement; Initiation Science* (CW 227) (in England at the Penmaenmawr Summer School); *The Four Seasons and the Archangels* (CW 229); *Harmony of the Creative Word* (CW 230); *The Supersensible Human* (CW 231), given in Holland for the founding of the Dutch society. On November 10, in response to the failed Hitler-Ludendorff putsch in Munich, Steiner closes his Berlin residence and moves the *Philosophisch-Anthroposophisch Verlag* (Press) to Dornach. On December 9, Steiner begins the serialization of his *Autobiography: The Course of My Life* (CW 28) in *Das Goetheanum*. It will continue to appear weekly, without a break, until his death. Late December–early January: Rudolf Steiner re-founds the Anthroposophical Society (about 12,000 members internationally) and takes over its leadership. The new board members are: Marie Steiner, Ita Wegman, Albert Steffen, Elisabeth Vreede, and Günther Wachsmuth. (See *The Christmas Meeting for the Founding of the General Anthroposophical Society*, CW 260). Accompanying lectures: *Mystery Knowledge and Mystery Centres* (CW 232); *World History in the Light of Anthroposophy* (CW 233). December 25: the Foundation Stone is laid (in the hearts of members) in the form of the 'Foundation Stone Meditation.'

1924: January 1: having founded the Anthroposophical Society and taken over its leadership, Rudolf Steiner has the task of 'reforming' it. The process begins with a weekly newssheet ('What's Happening in the Anthroposophical Society') in which Rudolf Steiner's 'Letters to Members' and 'Anthroposophical Leading Thoughts' appear (CW 26). The next step is the creation of a new esoteric class, the 'first class' of the 'University of Spiritual Science' (which was to have been followed, had Rudolf Steiner lived longer, by two more advanced classes). Then comes a new language for Anthroposophy—practical, phenomenological, and direct; and Rudolf Steiner creates the model for the second Goetheanum. He begins the series of extensive 'karma' lectures (CW 235–40); and finally, responding to needs, he creates two new initiatives: biodynamic agriculture and curative education. After the middle of the year, rumours begin to circulate regarding Steiner's health. Lectures: January–February, *Anthroposophy* (CW 234); February: *Tone Eurythmy* (CW 278); June: *The Agriculture Course* (CW 327); June–July: *Speech Eurythmy* (CW 279); *Curative Education* (CW 317); August: (England, 'Second International Summer School'), *Initiation Consciousness: True and False Paths in Spiritual Investigation* (CW 243); September: *Pastoral Medicine* (CW 318). On September 26, for the first time, Rudolf Steiner cancels a lecture. On September 28, he gives his last lecture. On September 29, he withdraws to his studio in the carpenter's shop; now he is definitively ill. Cared for by Ita Wegman, he continues working, however, and writing the weekly installments of his *Autobiography* and *Letters to the Members/Leading Thoughts* (CW 26).

1925: Rudolf Steiner, while continuing to work, continues to weaken. He finishes *Extending Practical Medicine* (CW 27) with Ita Wegman.

On March 30, around ten in the morning, Rudolf Steiner dies

INDEX

abyss, 29
acoustics, 43
Adams, George. *See* Kaufmann
    (Adams), George
aesthetics, 70
ahrimanically, 25
alchemy, 108
America/American, 25–27, 65, 102
anatomist/anatomy, 40, 76
angels, 56, 138
Anglesey, 74, 78, 111
animal/animal world, 6, 24, 31–32, 36,
    57–59
    animal husbandry/reproduction,
        113, 117
anthropological/anthropology, 40, 106
anthropos, 157
anthroposophical/Anthroposophy, xi,
    xiii, 20–21, 23, 26, 29,
    42–43, 47–49, 64, 70, 74,
    79–80, 83, 85, 91, 106, 111,
    114, 126, 145, 150–151,
    156–157
    anthroposophical medicine, 82
    anthroposophical movement, 48,
        69–70, 80, 119, 121
    Anthroposophical Society, xi,
        48–49, 157
        London branch, 53
antimony, 83
antipathy, 32, 37
archai, 56
archangel, 56
arithmetic, 18
arrogance, 113, 124

artistic/arts, xi, 38, 43, 46–47, 73, 82,
    94, 98, 154
    naturalism, 47
    painting, 45–47
astral, 9, 74, 76, 78–79, 115, 127, 141
    body, 32–34, 36, 55–57, 133, 138,
        142
astronomy, 18, 60, 110, 135
astrophysics, 110
Atlantean, 59
automatic writing, 145
automaton, 54–55
awareness/conscious awareness, 31–32,
    34, 36, 38, 45, 47, 53, 55,
    64, 84, 101, 106–107,
    110–111, 120–121, 125–127,
    130–131, 140–142, 145, 148,
    151, 157
    artistic awareness, 47
    hyper-awareness, 151
    self-awareness, 54
awe, 6

balance/balanced, 38, 148
Baldur, 99–100
Baravalle, von, Dr, 73, 82
Basel, xi
beautiful/beauty, 37–40, 43, 46
belief, 149
Berlin, 155–156
Black Sea, 92, 97
blood system, 44, 55–56, 62, 94, 107,
    109, 152
Boehme, Jacob, 120, 135, 137–138
    Mysterium magnum, 135